AUTHENTIC LITERACY INSTRUCTION

Empowering Secondary Students to Become Lifelong Readers, Writers, and Communicators

BILLY EASTMAN • AMY RASMUSSEN

Solution Tree | Press

555 North Morton Street
Bloomington, IN 47404
800.733.6786 (toll free) / 812.336.7700
FAX: 812.336.7790

email: info@SolutionTree.com
SolutionTree.com

Visit **go.SolutionTree.com/literacy** to download the free reproducibles in this book.

Printed in the United States of America

Library of Congress Cataloging-in-Publication Data

Names: Eastman, Billy, author. | Rasmussen, Amy, author.
Title: Authentic literacy instruction : empowering secondary students to become lifelong readers, writers, and communicators / Billy Eastman, Amy Rasmussen.
Description: Bloomington, IN : Solution Tree Press, [2021] | Includes bibliographical references and index.
Identifiers: LCCN 2021032359 (print) | LCCN 2021032360 (ebook) | ISBN 9781949539899 (paperback) | ISBN 9781949539905 (ebook)
Subjects: LCSH: Language arts (Secondary) | Language arts (Middle school) | Student-centered learning.
Classification: LCC LB1631 .E32 2021 (print) | LCC LB1631 (ebook) | DDC 428.0071/2--dc23
LC record available at https://lccn.loc.gov/2021032359
LC ebook record available at https://lccn.loc.gov/2021032360

Solution Tree
Jeffrey C. Jones, CEO
Edmund M. Ackerman, President

Solution Tree Press
President and Publisher: Douglas M. Rife
Associate Publisher: Sarah Payne-Mills
Managing Production Editor: Kendra Slayton
Editorial Director: Todd Brakke
Art Director: Rian Anderson
Copy Chief: Jessi Finn
Senior Production Editor: Laurel Hecker
Content Development Specialist: Amy Rubenstein
Copy Editor: Jessi Finn
Text Designer: Laura Cox
Cover Designer: Abigail Bowen
Editorial Assistants: Sarah Ludwig and Elijah Oates

For Violet and Atticus and all of the other writers of our next generation.

—B. E.

For Curtis, who always says I can.

—A. R.

ACKNOWLEDGMENTS

I thank my family members who have helped me grow into a writer and the person that I am today, especially Rachel, Atticus, Violet, my parents, and my siblings. It's such a wonderful gift to have people in your life who know more about you than you can even imagine at the time—the gift blossoms when you discover the truth they've always known.

Thanks to my friends, colleagues, and mentors who influence, challenge, and encourage me while I continue to grow and learn. Friends like Diane, JoAnn, Peg, and Susan have been instrumental mentors in the most meaningful of ways—I wouldn't be where I am today without their guidance. Additionally, numerous colleagues in Clear Creek Independent School District have pushed my thinking, grown alongside me without fear, and remained incredible friends all along the way.

I've been fortunate to spend time with master educators over the years: giants like Doug Fisher, Penny Kittle, Ernest Morrell, Lucy Calkins, Mary Ehrenworth, Lester Laminack, Alfred Tatum, and on and on. Whether you know it or not, each of you has shaped me as an educator, and I'm thankful for your tireless work that forever impacts the lives and futures of so many.

To the editing and production team at Solution Tree, a mountain of gratitude for guiding us through this book as first-time authors. Claudia, I'll always be grateful for your initial push.

Finally, to my coauthor Amy: it's been quite the journey! Thank you for embarking on it with me and being so kind, thoughtful, and persistent throughout the process. You are an amazing educator and even more amazing human.

—Billy Eastman

The first time I wrote something I thought someone might want to read was two years after I graduated high school. My best friend Connie had gone to Baylor University, and I was heading off to attend Weber State in Utah. As high schoolers, we had pulled some pranks—which we called dastardly deeds (nothing nefarious, just fun with our group of friends)—and I decided to chronicle them as a birthday gift for my friend. I wrote for days, typing story after story, detailing all the who, what, where, and when I could remember. I printed the pages and found a slim three-ring notebook for the binding. Connie said this "book" was the best birthday gift she'd ever received. "Now I'll always remember our adventures," she said. Maybe she did.

About midway through writing this book, I received news that Connie had died of brain cancer. She and I hadn't talked in almost two decades, and I can't even tell you why, other than that distance and the busyness of family, career, and illness (this wasn't Connie's first cancer) can do a number on a high school friendship. Accompanied only by regret, I attended Connie's memorial service and met her daughters. "You're Amy," they said. "You're the one who wrote the book—the book about the fun y'all had in high school. We just read it last night! It's so good to meet our mom's best friend!" I had completely forgotten I'd written those senior-year stories.

But stories live forever, and writing heals in more ways than one. I thought Connie would be the only one to read that little book, but more than thirty years later, her daughters found a moment of joy in their grief. I have to believe Connie is happy I'm writing still. She was the best at cheering teenage me onward.

So many of the best administrators, mentors, colleagues, students, friends, and family have cheered on adult me. They've pushed my thinking, challenged my practice, given me feedback, opened doors of opportunity, and tempered my drive to always do more as they've helped me learn to do better. To the following, I hope you know you're on my List of Bests, and I sincerely thank you for everything! So many of the ideas I share in this book and call my own no doubt came from others who've shared with me, taught and learned with me, and influenced and shaped my thinking. I hope my words do your work justice.

Georgeanne Warnock, whose gracious leadership and trust paved my early-career path. Penny Kittle, who taught me how to Write the World and smiled as I sobbingly read my writing on the first day of class. Penny taught me how to trust myself as I trusted her work and the work of other mentors who have researched, written, presented, taught, and shaped the work of authentic literacy instruction. Thank you for introducing me to the work of Louise Rosenblatt, Donald Murray, and Don Graves, and thank you for telling me I should attend Tom Newkirk's final class at the University of New Hampshire Literacy Institute. You gave me gold when you wrote "Go go go" on that first draft of what I thought would become my book. And, Penny, thank you for building a classroom community that summer of 2013. All of my classmates at #UNHLit13 sit high on my List of Bests, especially Shana Karnes, Erika Bogdany, and Emily Kim who helped me find my zen while eating ice cream at the Dairy Bar, walking on the beach in Maine, hiking in those beautiful White Mountains, and sharing the thoughts we penned in our notebooks every day in class. Thank you for writing beside me and showing me how to write beside students. North Star of TX Writing Project, especially teacher consultant Heather Cato, my first blog partner and don't-be-afraid-of-technology teacher. Amber Counts, Mary Davenport, and Joseph Gonzalez, who put up with my control issues as student teachers and now inspire students daily to own their learning. I knew you were diamonds from the get-go. ThreeTeachersTalk.com and all the contributors, especially my dear friends, fellow blog administrators, writing partners, and life coaches Shana Karnes and Lisa Dennis—and all the readers who care what we have to say about literacy. Donna Friend and the incredible English Department at Hebron High School, who welcomed me back to where I first started and provided a safe space to heal my soul and write a lot of this book. And my students throughout the years—all unique and talented individuals who've given me hope as you've shared your writing. You will live in my heart forever—especially you, Marcus, and you, Kimi and Biak, and my small senior English class of eight in the fall of 2019.

Finally, I am educated and an educator because of my family. Thank you, dear ones, for lighting my life with humor, wisdom, and wonder. You tackled responsibilities beyond your years when I returned to college. You loved and served one another when I was absorbed with my work. You supported my travels as I attended conferences and conducted trainings. Curtis, you are The Best: husband, friend, counselor, companion, thinking partner, and ghostwriter. Lauren, Josh, Tanner, Sarah, Jenna, Ryan, Kelly, Devin, Hyrum, and Zachary, you are the best of me—and you are my favorite. And grandkiddos—Julian, Linden, Elle, Quade, Dominic, Quillan, Indiana, Xavier, and Rocky, you—my precious little humans—you are the reason I advocate for authentic literacy instruction. I am better because of you. The world is better because of you.

—Amy Rasmussen

Solution Tree Press would like to thank the following reviewers:

Kasha Duff
English Teacher
Elgin Park Secondary School
Surrey, British Columbia, Canada

Nicholas A. Emmanuele
English Teacher and Department Chair
McDowell Intermediate High School
Erie, Pennsylvania

Charles Ames Fischer
Education Consultant
Decatur, Tennessee

Penny Gaither
Education Consultant
Minds Matter, LLC
Bloomington, Indiana

Michelle Rickicki
Professional Development and ELA Curriculum Coordinator
Friendship Central School District
Friendship, New York

Chad Stebbins
English Teacher
National Trail High School
New Paris, Ohio

Carrie Varnell
English Teacher
Oak Ridge High School
Conroe, Texas

Dawndy Zinnert
Language Arts Teacher
Benton Middle School
Benton, Louisiana

Visit **go.SolutionTree.com/literacy** to download the free reproducibles in this book.

TABLE OF CONTENTS

Reproducibles are in italics.

ABOUT THE AUTHORS

Billy Eastman is a curriculum coordinator for secondary English language arts in Clear Creek Independent School District in Texas, where he leads efforts to implement student-centered authentic literacy practices. He is a former curriculum specialist for secondary English language arts and high school English teacher in Fort Worth Independent School District, also in Texas. In 2017, he served on a Texas State Board of Education committee to write the state's new English language arts standards. Eastman has been an educator since 2008, serving as a teacher, curriculum supervisor, and professional development leader. His educational experiences range from a predominantly low-income majority-minority high school to one of the most progressive and influential school districts in Texas.

Eastman is a member of the National Council of Teachers of English (NCTE), the International Literacy Association (ILA), and the Texas Association of School Administrators (TASA). Additionally, Eastman serves as the president-elect for the Coalition of Reading and English Supervisors of Texas (CREST). He has been published in NCTE's *English Journal* and has presented at educational conferences across the United States on topics ranging from developing a culture of authentic literacy in secondary schools to implementing effective summer literacy programs. Eastman has also worked with schools and leaders to significantly invest in building teacher expertise through intensive professional learning institutes.

Eastman received a bachelor's degree in English from the College of the Ozarks in Missouri and a master's degree in curriculum and instruction with an emphasis in literacy studies from the University of Texas at Arlington.

To learn more about Eastman's work, follow @thebillyeastman on Twitter.

Amy Rasmussen is a literacy evangelist, consultant, writer, and education blogger. She specializes in supporting English language arts teachers as they embrace authentic literacy practices that help secondary students grow in their identities as readers, writers, and communicators. She has spent her career primarily serving marginalized populations in North Texas, including teaching high school English courses, writing curriculum, working as an instructional coach, and leading teacher teams.

Rasmussen is a teacher consultant of the National Writing Project. She is a member of the National Council of Teachers of English (NCTE) and has served on various NCTE committees, presented at multiple annual conferences, and been published in the *English Journal*. She is also a past president of the North Texas Council of Teachers of English Language Arts and a member of the International Literacy Association (ILA). In 2017, she served on a Texas State Board of Education committee for writing Texas's English language arts and reading standards. Rasmussen has facilitated a wide range of teacher trainings, with a focus on increasing student engagement in reading and writing, in many districts throughout the United States.

Rasmussen earned a bachelor's degree in English literature and a master's degree in secondary education from the University of North Texas. She continues to seek opportunities to improve her expertise as a literacy teacher and has taken several graduate-level courses at the University of New Hampshire Literacy Institute.

To learn more about Rasmussen's work, visit ThreeTeachersTalk.com or follow @amyrass on Twitter.

To book Billy Eastman or Amy Rasmussen for professional development, contact pd@SolutionTree.com.

INTRODUCTION

This book is based on hope. When we first started teaching, we had a lot of it. We chose to become English teachers because we liked our English classes as students and had (mostly) positive experiences in them: we read the books teachers assigned, and we wrote essays to their prompts. We didn't know anything different, so when we entered our careers, we taught in similar ways to how we were taught: we chose books for our students to read—primarily plucked from the canon—and we assigned writing—primarily with prompts about the literature. We engaged students in activities around the reading and writing. We did very little to grow authentic readers and writers.

Within a short time, we knew there had to be a better way. Our students weren't reading the assigned texts; they weren't writing as well as we knew they could write. Many were compliant, completing tasks to earn grades, but few showed genuine interest in their learning. We repeatedly sought out different tactics to increase engagement, but new strategies and activities designed to engage students or make learning relevant became harder and harder to come by. We were tired. Frustration festered. Was this really what teaching English language arts (ELA) was all about?

Hope kept us puzzling things out. We began asking soul-searching questions about our pedagogy, attending professional development, reading pedagogy-related books, and collaborating more effectively with other reflective educators. We had many conversations about *authentic literacy*, or what readers and writers do outside of school—things that keep them seeking out books and writing about their lives, learning, imagining, and wanting to improve their writing skills. These conversations planted the seeds of what it means to be authentic readers and writers and what that might mean for our teaching. We learned how choice in books and topics could lead to greater student engagement, which—together with modeling the moves of readers and writers—would lead to greater student learning. We attended summer institutes at the National Writing Project and Teachers College, Columbia University, and learned to become writers and to share our writing in communities of other writers. We started reading contemporary and young adult (YA) literature and talking about books with other readers. The more we developed ourselves as accomplished readers and writers, the more all this learning fueled the hope we had in our students and in our abilities to teach them in authentic ways with authentic tools and texts. In short, we changed, and we changed our teaching.

During this time in our careers, we found that "virtually all the authoritative voices and documents in every teaching field [were] calling for schools that are more student-centered, active, experiential, authentic, democratic, collaborative, rigorous, and challenging" (Zemelman, Daniels, & Hyde, 2005, p. vii). When we worked together on the committee for writing Texas's ELA and reading standards and realized our goals aligned so closely, we decided to join forces—bringing our knowledge and experience working with students in the Dallas–Fort Worth and Houston areas—and collaborate as we sought to answer the question, What does student-centered, active, experiential, authentic, democratic, collaborative, rigorous, and challenging teaching actually look like schoolwide and in individual secondary ELA classes? Seeking answers to that question led to our asking even more questions, such as:

> - Are we studying the research and evidence-based practices known to work in literacy learning and giving teachers and students time to practice them?
> - Are we concerned we have masses of high school students completely disinterested in education, unable to see the relevance of subjects taught [specifically literacy] to their lives?
> - Are we intentionally designing opportunities for teachers and students to enrich expertise with their craft—or merely expecting compliance and results? (Rasmussen & Eastman, 2018, p. 26)

Amy changed her instruction and started implementing classroom routines that invited students to become readers and writers, not just students going through the motions of completing school work. Billy, working as a district ELA supervisor, started sharing his experiences as a reader and writer and modeling authentic skills-based teaching for the teachers he supported. We gathered evidence that showed greater student engagement and greater teacher enthusiasm—authenticity was key.

In December 2016, we began transforming literacy learning systemwide in the large South Texas district of approximately forty-two thousand students where Billy works as a supervisor for ELA and reading. Since 2010, Amy had been sharing what was working with her high school students in North Texas at conferences, on her blog, and in various trainings, so Billy consulted her as he thought through the needs of the teachers and students in his district and how best to accomplish the goals set by his leadership team. Ultimately, this partnership led to Amy facilitating hands-on workshops for teachers with Billy and his core team of instructional coaches as they implemented authentic ideas and practices into their daily work. In the summer of 2017, with full support of district leadership, together we combined authentic literacy teacher training with student summer learning in our first three-week literacy institute, transforming professional development for teachers and remediation approaches for students (see Rasmussen & Eastman, 2018).

To do this work, we looked at the landscape of ELA classrooms districtwide, and we noticed some things needed to change. We noticed that student compliance outweighed student engagement. Instruction was either teacher centered or text centered with little concern for students themselves. And, of course (although we hate to even say the word *test*), standardized test scores were flat. Based on our research into student- and skill-centered instruction, changes we'd made in our own instructional routines with students, and the outcomes these changes had produced, we knew we could transform literacy learning systemwide, to the benefit of students and teachers across the district.

We also knew a shift of this magnitude would work only if teachers wanted it. Individual teacher and systemwide change would require *collective efficacy*, which is John Hattie's concept of "the collective belief in teachers in their ability to positively affect students" (Waack, 2018). We could not build collective efficacy toward improving literacy learning if we didn't trust teachers. No strict top-down curriculum. No unfunded mandates. We would meet teachers where they were and empower them to see the need for change themselves—and then teach, model, and help them learn how to satisfy that need.

We started with teacher expertise. As we had become writers in our summer institutes, our ability to teach student writers had grown exponentially, and we wanted this for our teachers. So we offered professional learning that tapped into teachers' lives, passions, and strengths, and in their own district-sponsored summer institute, our teachers became teacher readers and teacher writers. They owned these identities—just as we hope the students in their classrooms will year after year. Teachers began to stretch their thinking, take risks in their planning, and shift their practices to be more authentic. Most teachers achieved the transfer of skills we hope for with the students in our classrooms—some imitating our lessons exactly while others creatively expanded or ingeniously crafted their own—and we wanted to share this transformation with even more educators.

Of course, we did not do this work alone. Before we began, district administrators adopted objectives and crafted a strategic plan built on student interests and innovation. The district mission was clear:

> The mission of the Clear Creek Independent School District, the visionary leader igniting learning for all, is to ensure each student achieves, contributes and leads with integrity in a safe and nurturing environment distinguished by authentic relationships, service before self and the spirit of exploration. (Clear Creek Independent School District, 2018)

We worked within these new district goals, returning to our initial guiding question, and wondered how to take the macro mission (district and schools) into the micro mission (secondary ELA classrooms). That's where we knew our experiences could impact teacher expertise, thus impacting student expertise. So, again, we asked questions: How can we capitalize on student interests? What does authentic and practical innovation look like in English education? How does choice affect instruction? And finally, How do we put these ideas into sustainable action for teachers and for learners?

The answers to these questions led to districtwide implementation of a curriculum centered on authentic literacy practices, thorough teacher training through multiweek summer institutes, and funds spent on building vibrant, inclusive, high-interest classroom libraries. As a result, the majority of secondary ELA teachers in the district have become authentic literacy practitioners who model collective efficacy in their daily work with their teams and with their students. They take risks, step into vulnerable places as teacher readers and writers, center instruction on the individual needs of their learners, encourage students to grow from where they are, welcome choice and collaborative learning, and keep the focus on what real readers and writers do as they grow in their craft. "They do all that?" you might ask. "Yes," we will tell you, "that and more—because they know they can, and they choose to!"

In *Visible Learning for Literacy, Grades K–12: Implementing the Practices That Work Best to Accelerate Student Learning*, Fisher, Frey, and Hattie (2016) state this challenge:

> Teachers, we have choices. We can elect to use instructional routines and procedures that don't work, or that don't work for the intended purpose. Or we can embrace the evidence, update our classrooms, and impact student learning in wildly positive ways. (p. 33)

In this book, we share how authentic literacy instruction ensures these wildly positive outcomes.

As you read this book, you may recognize some of the terms we use, such as *mentor text*, *minilesson*, *conferring*, *writers' notebooks*, and *classroom library*. If you do, you may wonder why we don't just call the methodology we espouse *readers-writers workshop*. It sounds like it, doesn't it? The answer is simple: the term *workshop* means many things to many people, even those in literacy education. Some believe a workshop methodology means students rotating from station to station; others interpret workshop to mean a unit of study; others believe it comes in a box and can be swapped out for a binder with all the worksheets needed to teach a unit on *The Scarlet Letter*. We interpret workshop instruction to mean students doing the work: students working on skills to become better writers and reading books they choose to read for enjoyment, for learning, and as a means to become better readers. Perhaps you agree with this interpretation. Many do. However, preconceived ideas, even about a term like *workshop*, can interfere with learning, so we opted to write about how we've implemented readers-writers workshop and refined it to use the language, practices, resources, and habits of mind of readers and writers who identify as such, not just those participating in "workshops" in their English classes.

This book is for anyone working with secondary students, grades 6–12, to help them develop comprehensive and effective reading, writing, listening, and speaking skills. Your job title might be reading or writing teacher, literacy specialist, instructional coach, or English teacher. This book is also for literacy leadership teams or grade-level teams or departments and may serve as an important book study. We've designed this book to help you have critical conversations with others doing the weighty work of teaching adolescent readers and writers.

In chapter 1, we define *authentic literacy* and *authentic literacy instruction*. We explain how the implementation of this methodology revolves around three primary objectives: (1) teaching responsively to students' lives, cultures, interests, needs, and intrinsic motivations; (2) connecting reading, writing, listening, and speaking; and (3) crafting instruction that develops students' identities as real readers, writers, and communicators. Then, we present an authentic literacy action plan to help you reach these objectives. This action plan informs the topics of the remaining chapters.

Chapter 2 is all about growing your own expertise, as in practicing your role as teacher reader and teacher writer. In our experience, until individual teachers develop their own literacy expertise and share personal experiences and examples with their students, true and lasting change in instructional practice rarely takes firm enough root to withstand the demands of this work. Credible and trustworthy teachers must align their values and beliefs as literacy teachers with their literacy instruction. In this chapter, you'll learn how to craft this alignment and model the choices you make as a reader and writer. In essence, you do the things you ask your students to do, all while making your thinking visible. This requires risk taking and vulnerability, but we include ideas to help you develop your skills, and many of these same ideas you can use with students.

In chapter 3, you'll learn about building the relationships that create a community of authentic readers and writers. Adolescents crave a place to belong (in fact, we all do). English classes with a clear focus on the needs of individual learners can be safe havens of inclusive and equitable learning. You'll learn how to help students feel safe, welcome, and validated. You'll learn the difference between student engagement and student compliance, and what an engaged community of readers and writers looks like in secondary English classrooms. Finally, you'll learn practical ways to build community, set expectations, and gather information about your students.

Chapter 4 is all about choice and authentic engagement. Students' engagement soars when teachers offer them diverse, inclusive, highly engaging books they want to read, and invite them to explore their lived experiences as a means of choosing topics about which to write. We discuss how to guide students into making choices about their learning and how to leverage students' interests to foster engagement that leads to deep learning. Authentic literacy teachers do not need to rely on textbooks—they need to rely on their own expertise as readers and writers and on a classroom library filled with books adolescents want to read.

In chapter 5, we explore the qualities and practices that lead students to independently apply their literacy skills in new situations. Teachers can leverage factors like intrinsic motivation, student ownership, authentic inquiry, and purposeful struggle to ensure students develop as authentic readers and writers.

Chapter 6 discusses feedback and how effective feedback should always promote forward movement in a student's learning. We explain the functions of feedback, providing valuable information for improving instruction for individuals and the whole class.

Finally, in chapter 7, we describe effective literacy routines and detail what authentic literacy instruction can look like in daily practice. We review a number of strategies, with descriptors of teacher and student actions optimal for each routine. The routines are not rigid but will help guide you as you create your own daily agendas.

Each chapter also includes the following.

- An argument for an essential element of authentic literacy instruction
- Reflections From the Field on our personal experiences that describe the thinking we've done as we've worked to improve our craft as readers, writers, and authentic literacy teachers

- The rationale and research behind each topic, based on what we know about the needs of 21st century learners
- Practical ideas for implementing authentic practices related to the focus of the chapter
- Reader Reflection prompts that invite you (and your team or book study group) to process the ideas we share and reflect on your own practice
- End-of-chapter reproducibles for recording your action steps and refining your writing practice

As a whole, this book will guide and support you as you grow in your expertise as a reader, writer, and communicator, and as you shift your instruction to meet the needs, lived experiences, and interests of each learner. That's what all students deserve, and *that* is our best hope: authentic literacy instruction that weaves a transformative tapestry of opportunity for every student, every day, in every classroom (Allington & Gabriel, 2012).

CHAPTER 1

Authentic Literacy

Think about this for a moment: young people are creating massive amounts of literacy-related content—producing videos using iMovie and YouTube, posting on Instagram, designing video games. Many of them are intrinsically motivated to practice literacy *their* way. Yet they go to English class and get handed novels they have no interest in reading, prompts they have no desire to write about, and grammar packets they have little personal motivation to complete. Can you, as the teacher, give them something better? Can you apply the latest research and thinking to create more engaging ELA instruction? We know you can.

In this chapter, we define *authentic literacy* and its importance, and present an action plan for shifting your instructional practice toward authentic literacy.

Amy's Reflections From the Field

In my teaching career, I've experienced two powerful paradigm shifts: the first when I attended a three-week National Writing Project summer institute and realized I had been assigning writing, not teaching it; and the second when I attended the National Council of Teachers of English's annual conference in November 2016. I attended a session titled "Expert-to-Expert on the Joy and Power of Reading" with Kwame Alexander, Pam Allyn, Kylene Beers, and Ernest Morrell as panelists—all educators I admired. I took copious notes, but one thing Morrell said stayed with me:

> We are in a new classic movement in English language arts. It's a need for *right-now literature*: We need students to read like writers. To read and share their own genius in production. Students should be reading each other's works. They should be choosing their own books. (Alexander, Allyn, Beers, & Morrell, 2016)

Right-now literature. I couldn't help thinking about the imperative *right now*. After the conference, I looked into more of Morrell's work and found clarity in an interview he did with *English Journal* in 2012 (Gorlewski & Gorlewski, 2014). In it, he mentions "re-imaging" English education and explains re-imaging is, in part, a growing movement that asks tough questions in a quest to guide young people into the literacy practices needed to produce "self-actualizing, seriously literate students who are poised to become authentic and powerful participants in our multicultural democracy in the 21st century" (Gorlewski & Gorlewski, 2014, p. 15). I knew I was part of that movement. Morrell asserts in that interview, "We need to offer a different image of what is possible" (Gorlewski & Gorlewski, 2014, p. 15). It was onto this new image and possibility that I shifted my instructional focus. My focus no longer was pursuing *my quest*; it was helping my students have success on *theirs*.

What Authentic Literacy Is and Why It Is Important

Authentic literacy means identifying as a reader, writer, and communicator. It means doing the things effective readers, writers, and communicators do in their lives beyond school. It involves the intrinsic desires to read, explore, and discuss ideas; to make choices related to these desires; and then to write and talk about them. Perhaps shifting instruction toward authentic literacy seems idealistic, but shouldn't it be the goal of every secondary ELA teacher to help young people grow in their identities as readers, writers, and communicators?

Authentic literacy teachers are individuals who know the environment, circumstances, and skills students need in order to develop as effective readers, writers, and communicators because they identify as such themselves. These teachers read, write, and communicate as experts in their field, practicing the routines they hope their students will internalize as their own. And in order to teach authentically, they also do the following.

- Build relationships in communities of learners where every student feels seen, heard, validated, and celebrated.
- Facilitate conversations where all students feel safe and secure as they express ideas and opinions and learn to communicate, negotiate, and collaborate.
- Foster a love of books and reading based on choice, purpose, and accountability—and use these books to teach authentic literacy skills.
- Model the habits of mind and intentional moves of readers, writers, and communicators.

Authentic literacy instruction is skills-based instruction, modeled after what real readers, writers, and communicators do to improve their abilities and stretch their capabilities. Think about the content in an ELA class: the focus is primarily on skills—reading, writing, listening, speaking, and thinking. Teachers choose texts that aid in teaching these skills. That's where students' interests come in. Authentic literacy teachers design instruction clearly focused on their students and the lives they live—their cultures, customs, and personal histories—as the content that supports literacy acquisition.

In other words, authentic literacy instruction means that, in secondary ELA classes, the students drive the content. Students make choices about their learning—in the books they read, the topics they write about, and how they write about them. As a result, teachers meet students where they are; application becomes habit; transfer of skills in other contexts becomes possible; and all learners develop their identities as readers, writers, and communicators, prepared for whatever literacy-related tasks they may face in the future.

Many organizations have adopted Simon Sinek's advice of starting with their *why*. In his well-known TED Talk, Sinek (2009) presents the need to truly know your purpose, your cause, and your belief. He advises that you ask, "Why does your organization exist? Why do you get out of bed in the morning? And why should anyone care?" (Sinek, 2009). Many educators have taken this approach to teaching to heart, and determined their why, which is a great first step. However, Lindsey Gunn of the Cambrian Group takes Sinek's thinking a step further. Relating the concept to education, Gunn (n.d.) suggests educators should start with *who*. In the profession of educating young adults, you can ask yourself the same questions that Sinek asks. But if asked and answered honestly, the questions redirect educators from why to who. In an industry devoted to developing humans, the who must precede the why. Your purpose, your cause, your belief, why you exist, why you get out of bed in the morning, and why anyone should care are all wrapped up in the who: the individual young adults who need essential literacy skills to be prepared for life beyond the classroom.

In this way, learner-centered teaching is like writing. A good writer starts with the audience—the who—in mind. The intended audience influences the decisions the writer makes about every aspect of the writing process, from form to structure, syntax to word choice, and so on. Writers craft specific pieces of writing for specific audiences. In teaching, the students are the audience. They are the who. See "Sharpening the Focus on Your Who" to reflect on your own students' lives and literacy needs.

Reader Reflection: *Sharpening the Focus on Your Who*

By starting with your who, you will be better equipped to design instruction that meets the needs of your individual learners. Focus on the students you greet in your classroom each day as you reflect. The following questions will help you set your intention for literacy instruction. Share answers to these questions in your team or book study group.

- What do you know about your students' lives, cultures, and families?

- How do your students spend their time when not in school? What are their interests?

- When it comes to reading, writing, and communicating, what do you know about your students?

- What reading, writing, and communicating skills do young people need to navigate their lives beyond school?

Visit ***go.SolutionTree.com/literacy*** *for a free reproducible version of this reflection.*

While this approach to literacy instruction takes concerted effort and time, it produces lasting results. Learning thrives when teachers tap into students' intrinsic motivation to explore, grow, and adapt (Kohn, 1993, 2018). In order to capitalize on this, teachers should begin by paying attention to the things that are relevant, meaningful, and interesting to each individual learner (Guthrie & Wigfield, 2018). When you design instruction that sparks curiosity and builds on your students' intrinsic motivations, you aid them in applying the sophisticated, intersecting literacy skills they need to navigate this increasingly digital and complex world. They begin to take ownership of such skills and wield them purposefully in the tasks they do in school—and outside of it.

In the sections that follow, we present three essential features of authentic literacy instruction. Teachers should strive to design instruction that achieves the following.

1. **Knowing about and responding to students' lives:** Teachers should learn about students' cultures, interests, needs, aspirations, and intrinsic motivations and craft instruction that responds to them.
2. **Connecting reading, writing, listening, and speaking:** These skills cannot be separated from one another. Integrated literacy instruction is more realistic, requires a deeper level of critical thinking, and develops more sophisticated application of each skill.
3. **Developing students' identities as authentic readers, writers, and communicators:** The ultimate goal of literacy instruction is for students to internalize the skills and apply them beyond the classroom (Newkirk & Kittle, 2013).

Knowing About and Responding to Students' Lives

To design authentic literacy instruction, teachers need to meet their students where they are. Educators can celebrate what students bring to the table and foster their strengths, interests, and motivations toward growth in literacy skills. Each learner is a mosaic of cultures, beliefs, experiences, and interests. Yet traditional ELA instruction often ignores students' individuality rather than validating and utilizing it.

Instead of beginning with who learners are and what they can do, educators have traditionally obsessed over where they think learners should be. Donald Murray, the Pulitzer Prize–winning writer who started the University of New Hampshire journalism program and esteemed author of several books on writing and teaching, exposes this problem in his 1972 essay "Teach Writing as a Process Not Product":

> We teach English to our students as if it were a foreign language. Actually, most of our students have learned a great deal of language before they come to us, and they are quite willing to exploit that language if they are allowed to embark on a serious search for their own truth. (p. 14)

While Murray wrote about this issue—ignoring the personal interests, goals, identities, and cultural backgrounds that engage students—as it relates to the writing process, teachers often create the same problems with teaching readers. Traditionally, ELA teachers assign the "important" books from what they commonly refer to as the *canon*. They assign books instead of engaging readers with books they want to read—books that validate students' lives and experiences or help them discover their own truth. Fortunately, a wide variety of books relate to students' identities, cultures, and experiences. And students are reading them (Beach & O'Brien, 2018).

The Poet X by Elizabeth Acevedo (2018) and *On the Come Up* by Angie Thomas (2019), for example, both feature teenage protagonists who are caught in the maelstrom of who society says they should be and who they truly are. These are books that explore self-censorship, self-discovery, and so much more. These are books that highlight the need for teachers to craft instruction that develops learners' identities. Jason Reynolds, award-winning author of *Long Way Down* (2017), *All American Boys* (Reynolds & Kiely, 2015), *As Brave as You* (2016), and many other books, read his first novel at the age of seventeen, even though he had written original poetry from a young age. Reynolds says that too often, teens are bored with the books they are required to read because they don't see themselves in these books (University of Wisconsin–Madison School of Education, 2018). When he was a teen, he saw himself in rap music and then, finally, in *Black Boy* by Richard Wright (1945). His example highlights the need to provide students with access to books that meet them where they are, draw them in, and push them up.

Teachers can think through some of the lived experiences students may relate to as they try to fill libraries and help students find books that may interest them. Depending on where you live in the world and the young people you work with, ideologies and issues may vary, but growing into adulthood can be a tumultuous time. Of course, when considering your students' lives and asking them to explore memories as a means of getting to know them, be cautious of triggers. The last thing you want to do is force students to revisit trauma or induce more. They may tell you things when they are ready—or they may not. The students determine the depth of the relationships teachers create with them, and teachers must honor and respect them as they share in their own ways and on their own terms.

Respecting students' desires not to read, or write, may be equally important. Many students are disengaged from school. Many think of reading as a chore, rather than a pleasurable freedom that can help them explore places and experience events they may never get the chance to. Many think they have nothing to say, so why should they write? Remember, "Every writer—student or professional—comes to the page with a personal history as a human being and as a writer" (Murray, 1982, p. 55). This idea applies to readers, thinkers, and communicators as well. Your task is to tap into students' interests, motivations, and personal feelings about themselves as learners. To learn how students see themselves, help students find reasons to read and help them see books as allies instead of enemies (Kittle, 2013). When students are engaged with fascinating, relatable stories like those of Acevedo, Thomas, and Reynolds, learning about the young humans in your classroom becomes much easier.

Connecting Reading, Writing, Listening, and Speaking

Students of secondary literacy deserve instruction that does the following.

- Builds on their foundational skills
- Promotes their comprehension

- Stimulates their responses
- Relies on their understanding of multiple genres
- Activates their analysis and application of author craft
- Develops their composition skills
- Engages their capacity to practice inquiry and research ideas and issues

All these actions prove more fruitful when instruction integrates reading, writing, listening, and speaking as reciprocal skills. "Reading and writing are mutually supportive processes" (Laminack & Wadsworth, 2015, p. vii), as are listening and speaking. When ELA teachers teach reading or writing or communicating in isolation, they miss out on opportunities to teach students the reciprocal nature of authentic literacy skills. Readers are often better writers; writers are often already readers. Of course, there are exceptions—students who develop as readers much faster than they do as writers, and students who excel at writing but fake their way through book after book. These exceptions do not discount the importance of integrated reading and writing instruction.

Authentically integrated literacy instruction views reading and writing as two sides of the same coin: What choices does the author of the work you are reading make to craft meaning? What choices will you, student writer, make as you craft meaning? Using narrative as an example, figure 1.1 details how this works.

The same ideas shown in this graphic apply to other genres as well. Writers make purposeful choices as they craft meaning, whether in novels, short stories, persuasive essays, poems, cover letters, news articles, and so on. Readers notice these purposeful choices as they determine meaning; then, they flip over the coin—they become writers, who purposefully make choices to craft meaning.

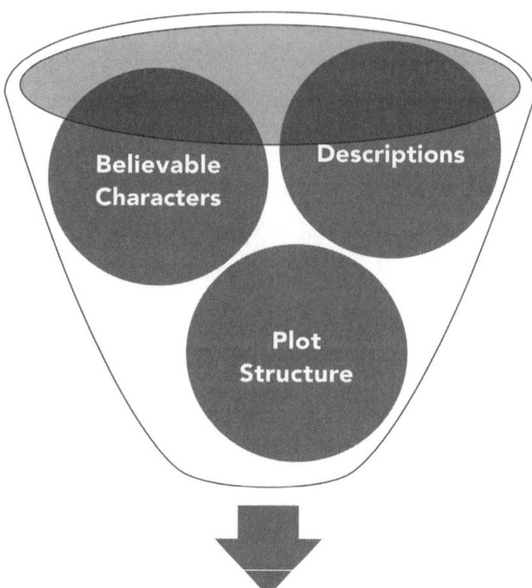

Reading: When we read, we learn to comprehend a text because we come to understand how language works to craft meaning. Authors make choices that create meaning.

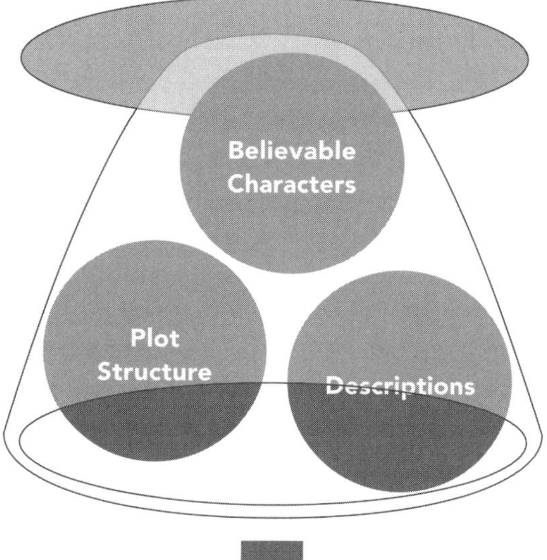

Writing: When we write, we create meaning for readers to comprehend, using what we know about how language works. We are the authors who make choices that create meaning.

Source: © 2021 by Tess Mueggenborg. Used with permission.

Figure 1.1: Integrated reading and writing instruction.

Listening and speaking come in throughout the learning process. Adolescent learners, for the most part, are social by nature, and talk is a vital component of a student-centered classroom. In the epilogue of the most recent edition of *Handbook of Research on Teaching the English Language Arts* (Lapp & Fisher, 2018), P. David Pearson and M. Lisette Lopez (2018) make "six claims about the current state of language and literacy instruction" (p. 451). The two of these claims that are particularly relevant here are as follows.

- "Engagement seems finally to be overtaking cognition as a central instructional driver" (p. 451).
- "Talk is a core, perhaps the core, practice propelling teaching and learning" (p. 451).

In an authentic literacy classroom, engagement and talk (listening and speaking) intertwine to strengthen the community and build culture. Regarding engagement, Pearson and Lopez (2018) synthesize the research, stating:

> The common finding . . . is that success in reading is not solely due to the acquisition of skills or the deployment of strategies but to promoting active, agentive, engaged learners who are motivated to read, write, and think. Indeed it is this motivation that propels readers to be strategic and writers to be purposeful. (p. 455)

Teachers hope for these attributes in their learners and develop them when they utilize adolescent desires to be social (Guthrie & Wigfield, 2018).

In our experience, students engage more with texts they read, whether it's books they choose or short texts read as a class, when they are able to talk about them with their peers. Students write more and work to improve their writing skills when they have opportunities to share their ideas about topic and craft with their peers and receive feedback. When teachers position the class, instead of themselves, as the audience for student writing, students engage more meaningfully in the writing process. They are more apt to hold one another accountable as well. This accountability takes shape as students speak to one another about their reading and writing and listen to what their peers have to say. In addition, it's through shared talk that teacher-student and student-student relationships form, and these relationships build communities of trust that lead to classroom cultures where individual voices can be amplified.

For authentic literacy instruction to work, students need to be in close proximity so they can discuss as they learn. Try seating students in pairs or small groups and letting them choose their own seats. Yes, classroom management concerns may arise, but when you explicitly teach students to value talk as a component of their learning—and model what this talk looks and sounds like—in most circumstances you can make it work. When students only have one or a few students to talk with, teaching them how to discuss their learning can be less challenging and time consuming than trying to get them to speak aloud to the whole class. Small groups increase many students' willingness to participate, as well as make participation rates more equitable. If a student group isn't working, for whatever reason—somehow all shy students grouped together and just won't talk, or gregarious students talk too much or too readily get off topic—move them around. Walk the room, monitor your groups, and make changes that benefit the whole of your learning environment.

Of course, listening and speaking protocols must be taught and modeled, and teachers must be willing to give up control. Giving up control can take practice, concerted effort, and planning. Fundamentally, increasing talk in the classroom is a question of power. Pearson and Lopez (2018) pose valuable questions regarding this topic: "Who holds the power? Who controls the floor? Who decides who talks next and who not at all? How do these differences play out? How are they sustained and strengthened? What can be done to resist or counter them?" (p. 456). Asking these questions can help teachers evaluate the talk taking place in classrooms. As teachers move out of the spotlight, there are some students who will step right into it. And conversely, there are some students who will stay crouched in the corners, never sharing their thinking or ideas, never showing they have learned the speaking and listening skills. Ultimately, Pearson and Lopez (2018) call for more research, stating: "We need a pedagogy of reciprocal classroom dialogue, not just talk, and we need to understand how to achieve it on a large scale" (p. 58). We posit that authentic literacy instruction that places listening and speaking skills side-by-side with reading and writing is the solution.

Developing Students' Identities as Authentic Readers, Writers, and Communicators

While books and other materials that validate and empower students' diverse identities, interests, and motivating factors are an important consideration, the instructional decisions teachers make in the classroom are equally important. Teachers often ask us about the usefulness of strategies or tools they consider using with their students. We frequently ask them in response, "Is this tool or strategy something an authentic writer or reader would employ?" Their first reply is often, "Wait, what?" but we maintain it's a good question. If ELA teachers' goal is to develop real readers and writers, it makes sense that students would do in class what real readers and writers do, often on their own, to become better readers and writers. Answering this question helps teachers make instructional choices that are authentic to the subject.

Authentic literacy instruction has a place in every classroom. The unavoidable thing is, to move forward, you must leave some things behind. The answers to our question—Is this tool or strategy something an authentic writer or reader would employ?—will also help you determine what you must throw out to make space for essential authentic literacy.

So what are some of the things you can leave behind? Essentially, anything a real writer or reader wouldn't do in authentic reading and writing contexts. The stuff that people do *only* in school. The stuff that is more about compliance and less about empowerment. The teacher-centered stuff. The test-prep stuff. Whole-class novel studies that take up weeks of learning time. Assessments that focus on recalling information or simply summarizing lectures. The stuff that makes young adults say, "I can't wait to get out of school so I never have to read another book or write another paper." Literacy teachers aim to graduate young adults who are looking for the next reason to write and the next book to read. This is the goal because we desire a healthy, inclusive, democratic society for the future. Yes, authentic literacy is *that* big.

Table 1.1 lists some characteristics of authentic readers, writers, and communicators that we aim to foster in all students. You can use these characteristics as a litmus test of sorts as you design instruction that develops authentic literacy in students. Keep the lens of authenticity clearly focused on your specific students—your who—and plan, design, and deliver instruction in ways that develop young adults who can be proactive contributors in the ever-changing, often chaotic world in which they live. Which of these characteristics do you most often see in classroom instruction? Which do you rarely see?

Literacy teachers have the opportunity to teach young adults how to think, how to communicate, and how to analyze context for their own thinking and communication. See "Determining the Other Stuff" (page 16) to reflect on common but inauthentic classroom practices.

Table 1.1: Some Characteristics of Authentic Readers, Writers, and Communicators

Authentic Readers	Authentic Writers	Authentic Communicators
• Read for pleasure and for knowledge • Know the books they enjoy (topics, genres, authors) • Understand that some books may be too easy and other books may be too challenging • May choose to abandon books • Know strategies for comprehension • Make connections • Grow in background knowledge • Acquire a larger vocabulary • Understand that form, structure, grammar, and punctuation contribute to meaning • Take risks, stepping out of their comfort zones, as they participate in conversations in communities of other readers	• Enjoy exploring ideas in print • Understand that writing is thinking • Collect ideas (personal experiences, observations, conversations, snippets from others' writing) • Share ideas in communities of other writers • Recognize authors' craft in texts they read • Identify form and structure and play with them as they create meaning • Value revision as an opportunity for discovery • View editing as a service to their readers	• Understand the importance of listening • Employ listening strategies • Interpret nonverbal cues • Know how to give and receive feedback • Practice discussion protocols • Greet others with warmth and enthusiasm • Ask thoughtful questions and listen to understand, learn, and empathize • Take turns speaking and wait for others to finish speaking before interjecting ideas

Reader Reflection: *Determining the Other Stuff*

Think about tasks that secondary literacy teachers often ask students to do, but that are inauthentic to those who identify as readers and writers outside of school. Make a list of this "other stuff"—anything a real writer or reader wouldn't do in authentic reading and writing contexts. (We've included a couple of items to get you started.) Discuss your list with a colleague, or compare your list with those of your team or book study group members.

- Grammar worksheets
- Questions about characterization at the end of a short story, which students silently write down answers to
-
-
-

Visit ***go.SolutionTree.com/literacy*** *for a free reproducible version of this reflection.*

Billy's Reflections From the Field

Let me tell you about Charles, a football coach and English teacher. I met Charles within the first couple of months of working in my district position. I could tell after just a few brief interactions he cared deeply about growing young men as football players, and like most high school football coaches in Texas, that is where he put a great deal of his time and energy. Charles understood the value of authentic learning with kids on the football field: practicing plays again and again, responding to conflict, taking risks, making mistakes, giving feedback, and reflecting and revising before and after every game. In essence, he was always coaching. Charles understood that his athletes needed to find relevance in their hard work and develop habits of mind when it came to learning skills. That way, when it was game time and he stood coaching from the sidelines, his athletes could ultimately own the choices they needed to make when they were out on the field, far from his immediate reach and the sound of his voice.

So when Charles learned about authentic literacy instruction via a two-day training, several light bulbs went on for him. I saw his posture change, his focus shift from whatever he'd been thinking about, and his enthusiasm for learning the pedagogy just about launch him from his chair. Charles instinctively realized everything he knew from coaching football had a place in his English classroom: students needed to practice literacy skills again and again, they needed freedom to take risks and a safe place to make mistakes, and they needed feedback before, during, and after tasks. In essence, his English students needed Charles to act more like a coach.

With a personal investment in building his expertise as a literacy teacher and a framework for authentic instructional planning, Charles quickly began shifting his practice. His students needed much more time to read and write and talk than he had given them before, so he put some things to the side. Charles started to read books he thought his students would read. He began talking about these books so his students could see real readers talk about what they read. He shared the books he loved with me, so I could try to order them, and he shared titles with his colleagues. Charles also began writing with his students so his students could see the thinking of a writer. He posted personal poems on his whiteboard. He loved it all, and so did his students. The previously uninspired high school seniors in Charles's classroom started to regain a love of reading and a real purpose for writing. Some even found this love and purpose for the first time ever. And Charles celebrated these successes just like an excited football coach from the sidelines.

I personally observed the changes in this teacher. Charles will tell you the change he saw in his students came because he knew he could effect change if he walked the walk—and taught—as a reader and writer himself. And as Charles shifted his instructional practice, his identity as a reader and writer continued to grow—the exact effect he expected in his students.

If Charles's story ended there, I would still call it a win as an instructional leader, but since he started on this journey into authentic literacy learner, Charles has also become a contributing writer on Amy's blog, served in leadership for the Texas Council of Teachers of English Language Arts, completed his master's degree in education, and served as a district-level instructional coach. Charles no longer coaches football players. He coaches teachers and cheers them on as they embrace authentic literacy practices.

An Action Plan for Authentic Literacy

In *Visible Learning for Literacy*, Fisher and his colleagues (2016) begin, "Every student deserves a great teacher, not by chance, but by design" (p. 2). Authentic literacy work, however, does not come easy. It's an individual teacher's work, and it cannot be purchased as a unit or copied from a textbook—that would negate what it means to be an authentic literacy teacher who understands and practices becoming an expert reader, writer, and communicator in his or her own life. What works for you may not work for others. When it comes to literacy instruction, then, instruction must be personal to the teacher and flexible to meet the needs of diverse students.

As you transform your teaching, you will put research into practice by planning and implementing authentic literacy actions. The following list outlines our authentic literacy action plan in its simplest form. These practical steps open up time and space for actions to become daily routines, and those routines become personal habits for individual learners. Chapters 2–7 each provide more detail on one of these action steps.

1. **Own your literacy expertise:** Focus on and practice becoming the best reader, writer, and communicator in the room. As you internalize this self-development, plan instruction that shares your personal literacy practices with students. Make connections with other educators who stay current in literacy best practices.
2. **Create an optimal environment for readers and writers:** The classroom community welcomes trust, vulnerability, risk taking, and honest feedback and is steadfast in high expectations. Provide opportunities for individuals to share their wants, needs, desires, and motivations. Surround students with books they want to read, and provide comfortable spaces for them to write and collaborate.

3. **Allow your students to make choices:** Promoting student choice in the literacy classroom increases engagement and motivation. A robust classroom library allows learners to select books that interest them. Purposeful but open-ended writing opportunities let students experience the choices that authentic writers make. Of course, you will have to guide students to make good choices through modeling and targeted instruction.
4. **Prepare students to independently apply their literacy skills:** The ultimate goal is that students can and do transfer the skills they learn in the classroom to real life. Literacy teachers can prepare students to do this by fostering intrinsic motivation, student ownership, authentic inquiry, and productive challenges.
5. **Learn the language of effective feedback:** Almost every conversation with a student can be a teaching opportunity. Practice using language that validates your readers and writers, draws them into a discussion, allows them to express their needs, and feeds their literacy identities.
6. **Establish authentic literacy routines:** Use daily routines that center on reading, writing, listening, and speaking skills. These routines will form habits for all readers and writers.

Although there is always more to learn when it comes to developing as a reader, writer, and teacher, following this plan will help you become an authentic literacy expert in your own right. Discuss this action plan with your team or book study group. Make a note of questions you may have.

Summary

Authentic literacy means that you choose to lead your students by example. It means that if you haven't already done so, you begin identifying as a skilled reader and writer. Authentic literacy instruction focuses your preparation on your who—your students—and you meet them where they are by allowing them to drive the content. It means you will need to design your classroom to be more about their interests than yours. You'll have to get to know them better. You'll have to learn better ways to ask questions to connect with them. And you'll have to get them talking about what they think or feel. You'll see that engagement take off as you search for books they might enjoy. Perhaps a young man loves basketball, and he watches YouTube videos of old-school NBA players. You surprise him with a book written by Kareem or Shaq. (Watch how he talks about that book with the other students.) Maybe a young woman loves dancing, and you show her a list of twenty-five books about dancers, dancing, and so on. You customize this for every student in every classroom, but most important, you customize learning for you—sometimes you're the who. Imagine those amazing moments when you excitedly share your reading and writing discoveries with your students. Authentic learning comes together when you talk the walk, then walk the talk. You are transformed, and transformation happens for many of your students, too. You will see your students' respect for you rise—and they'll follow you in creating wildly positive outcomes for themselves and the world beyond the classroom! To begin this journey, the next chapter explores developing your own authentic literacy expertise.

Your Turn: Chapter 1

John Maxwell (2019) said, "We look back before we look ahead because reflection is the process that turns experience into insight," and writing about your experiences often reveals this insight in authentic ways. Choose one of the following questions to consider, and record your thinking. Then, find a partner or a team or book study member, and share your writing.

- Think about your own experiences as a student in secondary English language arts classes. Based on our definition of authentic literacy instruction, would you say the instruction you received was authentic? Why or why not?

- Recall writer Jason Reynolds's experience, which we mentioned in this chapter (page 11). How is it possible to advance through school without reading a book, particularly a novel in his English classes? Why might some individual students choose to write poetry but refuse to read the books assigned in school? What about you—did you read? What did you like to write?

- How might a focus on the individual students' strengths and challenges throughout the year shift the focus of what you prioritize instructionally?

CHAPTER 2

Teacher as Authentic Literacy Expert

Redefining yourself as an English teacher is the first step in transforming your practice to one of inclusive and authentic literacy. To tackle this transformation, you must become a student of the craft. When teachers grow in their own identities as authentic literacy learners, they become authentic literacy experts—the kind of teachers ELA students deserve.

Authentic literacy instruction requires responsiveness and exploration of new ideas, new books, and new ways of reaching and teaching to the lived experiences of your learners. This active and ever-evolving instruction is the crux of *critical literacy*—the act of readers' moving beyond traditional reading comprehension to read not only the word but also the world. Researchers and professors Maureen McLaughlin and Glenn DeVoogd (2018) recommend, "As literacy professionals we must . . . continue to view literacy instruction as a process of incessant discovery" (p. 104). Is this a discovery for only our students? We don't think so.

Authentic literacy instructors can practice the same vulnerability and discomfort that students often feel when trying new strategies and applying new skills. Instead of staying in the realm of comfort ("I've always done it this way"), proactively plan for new learning experiences even when you are not certain of the outcomes. In fact, Fisher and colleagues (2016) claim, "Errors should be the hallmark of learning—if we are not making enough errors, we are not stretching ourselves" (p. 31). It's OK to write poorly in front of colleagues and students. It's OK to not know all the answers about a text. Making mistakes when applying new learning in an authentic context is the best way to learn (more on this in chapter 5, page 78). Teachers put students in situations like this all the time, yet teachers themselves avoid them. Why? The usual answer is *credibility*, which is "a constellation of characteristics, including trust, competence, dynamism, and immediacy" (Fisher et al., 2016, p. 11). Maintaining credibility does not mean never making a single mistake. Indeed, by being real, by doing the tasks you ask your students to do, you increase the immediacy and dynamism of instruction, demonstrate trustworthiness to students, and develop your own competence as a reader and writer.

To grow in expertise as an authentic literacy instructor, you must seek the experiences in which you can grow. It's as simple as that. Teachers can begin transforming their individual identities as readers and writers by designing multiple opportunities to apply their own literacy practices in authentic contexts, both with colleagues in team meetings and with students as they read and write beside them. If you don't have colleagues you can practice reading and writing with, you do have students. This is what we mean by becoming an authentic literacy expert: with an investment in your own literacy learning, you can become the best reader, writer, and communicator in the room. Can it be unnerving, maybe even a little scary? Sure. Is it worth it? Absolutely.

In this chapter, we discuss shifting your conception of ELA instruction and present several strategies for building your own expertise.

Billy's Reflections From the Field

"Honestly, we don't know what this kind of teaching looks like."

This comment from the teachers I supported was the greatest welcoming gift I could have received as I started my new position as curriculum coordinator. Charged with implementing an instructional methodology in high school English classrooms that would produce significantly higher outcomes, I wondered where my teachers stood in their ability and willingness to adopt significant instructional shifts. I had an idea of the direction we should go and the steps we could take to get there, but I needed to know their thoughts and feelings—I refused to come into a new position and begin making demands. Change can be difficult, and I knew systemwide change would take concerted effort from everyone.

I knew relationships matter most in any attempt to create lasting change, so I started there. I talked to my teachers; then, I listened. I shared the charge I'd been given—and I tried to help them see the value of opening up space for student-centered authentic literacy practices that benefit both teachers and their students. They told me what they knew and what they didn't. They told me how they felt about past instructional changes, about the whims and fads that come and go. They told me of their frustrations but also of their hopes. I quickly got a sense of possibility, and when one teacher said, "We don't know what this methodology looks like," I knew where to start the shift of change.

A core team of six teachers, who also worked as part-time instructional coaches, and I started by visiting Amy's classroom in Lewisville, Texas. I knew her instructional practices epitomized the ideal authentic literacy classroom. She'd been practicing and refining this model for years. With district support, a team of teachers—hungry to learn and eager to see students learn in authentic ways—and I participated as Amy read with her students, wrote beside them, conferred with learners, and offered a wide variety of choices. We spent the day listening, experiencing, and questioning. My team left in awe at the high student engagement and burning with questions.

Back in my own school, I knew I had a responsibility to walk the talk I preached; I had to model everything I expected teachers to accomplish in their classrooms. I focused on building authentic relationships, displaying a love for reading and sharing my reading identity, writing with a purpose from my life, and celebrating what worked while revising what didn't. I spent time and energy promoting possibilities rather than dictating rigid mandates. In every professional learning opportunity, I taught the way I hoped my teachers would teach, modeling the moves of authentic literacy.

> It's very difficult to envision something you have never experienced. An authentic experience heightens authentic learning. This is one reason we advocate for an investment in teacher expertise. Our educational professionals deserve the time and expense of experience, especially if we expect authentic literacy habits to transfer to instructional norms within the classroom.

The Shift Beyond Traditional ELA Instruction

Far too often, secondary ELA is taught as a literature course. In many cases (including ours), English teachers become English teachers because of the literature they loved, a passion to share their favorite books and favorite authors with the next generation of readers. Less often, secondary ELA is taught as a writing course. Writing is assigned, composed, and assessed—mostly related to the literature being read or teacher-selected topics, forms, and structures. Students have little involvement in the delivery of instruction, except for the occasional writing conference. Educators and experts know these approaches don't work, yet they persist. Research on literacy best practices finds these common instructional approaches' lack of authenticity troubling: "The multi-decade gap between research and practice is a great concern" (McLaughlin & DeVoogd, 2018, p. 104). The world has changed significantly with the integration of technology, social media, easier access to high-quality texts and resources, global connectivity, and more—why does literacy instruction lag so far behind?

In our observations, interactions, conversations, and experiences, many secondary ELA classrooms continue to focus on teacher-selected texts from classic literature—the so-called canon. Most instructional time is devoted to teacher-centered lessons, with very little left for discussion and collaboration. Yet discussion and student-centered talk are crucial for developing academic knowledge and skills while promoting students' sociocultural and academic identities (Pearson & Lopez, 2018). Student choice also promotes engagement, comprehension, and literacy growth, including building students' personal identities and literacy habits (Skerrett & Warrington, 2018).

If research shows that the more reading experience learners have, the better readers they will become (Allington, 2013), then teachers must create systems and honor values that set their learners up to read as much as possible. If research shows that the more access learners have to a wide variety of texts, the better chance they will have for academic success (Skerrett & Warrington, 2018), then teachers must devote resources and create systems that increase access to diverse texts. To reflect on your own starting point for this shift, see "Charting Your Class Time" (page 24).

Reader Reflection: *Charting Your Class Time*

Think about your instruction on an average day in class. Then, create a graph that represents your answers to the following questions. Share and discuss your findings with your team or book study group members.

- What percentage of class time do you spend talking?
- What percentage of class time do students spend in discussion and academic talk?
- What percentage of class time do students spend reading?
- What percentage of class time do students spend reading something they chose for themselves?
- What percentage of class time do students spend writing?
- What percentage of class time do students spend writing something they chose for themselves?

Create your graph here.

What do these percentages tell you about your practice? Do they represent your understanding of current academic research on literacy instruction? Why or why not?

Visit ***go.SolutionTree.com/literacy*** *for a free reproducible version of this reflection.*

If the research is clear and compelling, why haven't more literacy teachers shifted their approach? There are numerous reasons, including lack of direct exposure to research and best-practice recommendations, personal affection for classic literary works, and insufficient training.

One barrier to research-backed changes in literacy instruction is teachers' limited time for and access to that research. We understand it can be intimidating to find time and resources to study the research that supports a shift to authentic literacy instruction. To start, you can refer to the citations and reference list (page 143) of this book. Buy or borrow a copy of the *Handbook of Research on Teaching the English Language Arts, Fourth Edition*, edited by Diane Lapp and Douglas Fisher (2018). Read it and take notes. Seek out the National Writing Project's (www.nwp.org) resources or local sites, and attend its workshops and institutes. Join the National Council of Teachers of English (https://ncte.org) and International Literacy Association (www.literacyworldwide.org), and subscribe to their newsletters and professional publications. What do these resources say 21st century students need?

Award-winning reading expert Cris Tovani (2016) presents two questions that can simplify the journey to align your practice with the research.

1. What are the beliefs that drive your practice?
2. What evidence supports these beliefs?

These are important questions for all educators, and especially important for those who believe they can make better choices about the instructional practices that prepare students for their futures. As you consider your beliefs, seek out authoritative information, put your learning into action in your classroom, and abandon long-held traditions that no longer work, you fill the gap between research and practice. Then, you start to have an effect on others, and—hopefully—they start filling the gap, too.

Every secondary ELA educator has the capacity to take the theory and research findings and turn them into classroom practice. But the most sustainable way to accomplish this shift is to move forward in community, preferably as colleagues set on transformation. Individual teachers may need to find companions who will join them on this journey, even if these companions are not in their department, on their campus, or in their school district. Like-minded teacher communities housed on social media are teeming with teachers making connections, sharing research and resources, and supporting one another in authentic literacy practices. Isolation is an enemy to innovation, and that applies to literacy practices as much as anything else. Joining a network wherein you can receive and share resources and ideas is easy and reduces the individual burden of finding and applying the research. See "Expanding Your Network" (page 26) to establish connections and grow a personal learning network.

Reader Reflection: *Expanding Your Network*

Pull out your cell phone, and take a few minutes to get connected or to expand your network. We suggest using Twitter because it makes it easy to tap into the thinking of respected teacher leaders and teacher researchers who focus on literacy instruction. Set up an account, and add a profile picture and a short bio (these show you are a real person and not a bot). Now, you are ready to get connected! Search for these people and organizations, and follow them.

- Solution Tree @SolutionTree
- Billy Eastman @thebillyeastman
- Amy Rasmussen @amyrass
- National Council of Teachers of English @NCTE
- International Literacy Association @ILAToday
- Poetry Foundation @PoetryFound
- Library of Congress @librarycongress

You may also want to find and follow:

- Your favorite bookstores
- Authors who write YA literature
- Bloggers who write reviews of YA books
- News sources and online magazines
- Other literacy teachers

If you look at the profile of a person you already follow, you can see who that person follows. This is a quick way to build your network. Use the search feature and hashtags to help you find other educators who share ideas and resources. Try #elachat, #teachlivingpoets, and #teachdiversetexts.

Consider the nature and importance of teacher communities. Record your thoughts, and discuss them with your team or book study group.

*Visit **go.SolutionTree.com/literacy** for a free reproducible version of this reflection.*

Another challenge in shifting instructional approaches to literacy is teachers' personal love for classic works of literature. In many cases, teachers who stick with tradition love the works of Shakespeare. They enjoy reading and sharing novels by Harper Lee, Charles Dickens, Mark Twain, Nathaniel Hawthorne, and Jane Austen, sometimes with a nod to Frederick Douglass or Zora Neale Hurston, or other "diverse" authors. Often, ELA courses centered on these works do not consider the cultures, lives, or reading levels of their students—or whether their students even read the assigned works. In our work with teachers, we've heard this a lot: "I love teaching *this book*." While affection for certain books does not in itself necessarily hold teachers back from implementing more authentic practices, we do believe it can harm the choices teachers make as they work to inspire students and help them develop their own reading identities. This doesn't mean we advocate abandoning the classics. Instead, we suggest a balance in the titles we introduce to our students and the choices we afford them. We also think it's wise to consider the voices we privilege in the texts we select. Whose voices do we leave out?

Some say that students must read the classics because those are the rigorous and complex texts. While we certainly want to guide students to read challenging texts, a text's being labeled a classic does not necessarily make it rigorous or challenging. On the other hand, a text does not necessarily lack rigor or complexity simply because it is contemporary or labeled YA. Ultimately, we agree with professors Corinne Bancroft and Peter J. Rabinowitz (2014) when they write, "What's significant is not the complexity of the text, but the complexity of the interpretive act you're performing" (p. 4). We shift the focus *from* the literature *to* the students we want to read it—the students who will perform that interpretive act.

For example, let's consider a single text—an excerpt from Rex Ogle's (2019) fantastic memoir for young adults, *Free Lunch*. Readers might read this text to identify with and respond to the author's experience with bullying in a Texas middle school. Readers could read the text to analyze what the author is saying about unhealthy environments in school. They might read the text to evaluate and emulate how the author creates tone. These tasks vary widely, but the complexity of the text didn't change; the complexity of the task did.

In another case, students may read the same text, let's say *The House on Mango Street* by Sandra Cisneros (1991), at different grade levels. This is natural, as real readers—even adults—have a habit of returning to texts and reading them again. But the interpretive task of reading the text will be more complex for students as twelfth graders than it was for them as seventh graders, simply due to the maturity and life experience gained in those five years. They will notice different things, think about different things, and want to talk about different things. Once again, the text didn't change in complexity; the task did because the older, more mature reader sees deeper meanings and notices more sophisticated writing craft moves that Cisneros makes.

Much of what makes literacy work rigorous is not the text but the interaction between the reader and the text. To quote professor Jeffrey D. Wilhelm (2015), "Interpretive complexity, or what the reader is doing with the text, should be the focus of our teaching. We don't teach texts! We teach specific human beings—our students—to engage with texts" (p. 46). Again, we are not saying to stop introducing classic literature to students. Depending on your students and their needs as learners, there may be a place for this literature, but to say teachers must teach any specific text to provide rigorous instruction is simply not true.

The final barrier to authentic literacy instruction we must discuss here is that teachers who stick with tradition lack the preparation and training necessary to bring literacy learning more in line with research-based recommendations. In far too few preservice courses do teachers learn what it takes to address the vast array of needs that student readers and writers have. Some teachers feel ready for classroom management, others for teaching novels or stories or poetry, but in our experience working with hundreds of new and expert teachers, few feel adept at teaching writing. And only a select few were fortunate enough to learn in programs that actually taught them in authentic ways how to teach authentic literacy skills. Fortunately, we know this is changing. Many university professors we consider mentors embrace authentic literacy instruction and model it as they prepare teachers for the classroom, including Sarah Donovan, assistant professor of secondary English education at Oklahoma State University (www.ethicalELA.com); Paul Thomas, professor of education at Furman University (www.radicalscholarship.wordpress.com); and Tom Romano, professor emeritus of English methods and writing at Miami University, who has written numerous books intent on teaching high school students how to write authentically. While changes to many university programs may still be needed, this topic is beyond the scope of this book.

No matter your initial training or reasons for choosing this profession, you can and may need to do more individual work to continue expanding your own expertise. Teaching readers and writers is not prescriptive. Authenticity does not lie in textbooks or curriculum guides or activities or lesson plans. You find it first within yourself as an authentic learner of your craft, and then you share and model and instruct your students in ways that help them find it in themselves. See "Developing Your Expertise" to reflect on where you are now and how you can grow your own practice.

Reader Reflection: *Developing Your Expertise*

All literacy teachers must develop their own expertise to prepare to develop their students'. How you answer the following questions may determine how much stretching you'll need to do. Write down your answers to these questions, and share your thoughts with your team or book study group.

- When did you last discover something new as a reader?

- When did you last discover something new as a writer?

- What investment have you made in your own literacy development?

- What do you call yourself—English teacher? Reading teacher? Writing teacher? Literature teacher? Literacy teacher? Depending on your answer, how might changing your title help you on your journey into gaining more authentic literacy expertise?

Visit ***go.SolutionTree.com/literacy*** *for a free reproducible version of this reflection.*

Some of the Ways Authentic Literacy Teachers Build Their Expertise

Every serious professional takes time to practice his or her craft. A scientist practices science. An artist practices art. The craft of teaching literacy demands that, as professionals, teachers routinely refine their own thinking, listening, speaking, reading, and writing. Becoming an authentic literacy teacher is a challenging business, and it's a challenge worth undertaking as you work to energize your students in the processes they require to develop literacy identities in their own right.

An authentic literacy teacher takes the following actions.

- Finds personal pleasure in the act of reading and understands the value of and purposes for writing
- Models the reading and writing habits of an expert reader and writer
- Instructs the individual readers and writers in the classroom, rather than teaching prescriptive texts and assigning prescriptive writing topics with prescriptive formulas

The subsequent sections detail each one. We encourage you to consider which strategies you might try and to record your primary action steps in the "Your Turn" reproducible at the end of the chapter (page 36).

Finding Personal Pleasure and Value in Reading and Writing

Think about your personal reading and writing life. Do you have one? If you do, how can you expand it? If you don't, how can you open space to read and write more?

Fostering a culture of readers in a community of learners first depends on teachers' having time to read and permission to value the time given to this task. If students are to discover a love of reading—the beauty, pleasure, and aesthetic value of it—then teachers must start by rediscovering (if they've lost it) the value in *aesthetic reading*—simply reading for the pleasure and the beauty found in books (Raines, 2005). As teachers practice authentic literacy, including reading for pleasure, sharing their reading lives, writing with purpose about things they care about, talking about books students want to read, and trading ideas, they grow in experience and confidence, both vital to implementing authentic literacy routines in their own classroom communities. They share the pleasure they gain from reading with their learners so students can see the joy that's possible when they read for pleasure.

We know you may have little time for "just reading," but the time teachers often use on many of the "adminis-trivia" tasks, such as turning in lesson plans, may prove less important than time to read and share their books, interests, epiphanies, disappointments, and more—and, then, to write about these things. Ideally, school leaders will dedicate time for teachers to read for pleasure, talk about books, and write from or about what they are reading during scheduled professional learning time. Reading for enjoyment or just for fun is direct evidence of intrinsic motivation (Guthrie & Wigfield, 2018), for teacher learners as well as students, and writing about reading can be equally motivational. If your leaders do not currently offer this time, we recommend that you advocate for this valuable use of time in your school. Can leaders allow for ten minutes of pleasure reading before other tasks on their agendas? We think so.

Individual teachers can also join reading communities digitally. Social media is perfect for this. You can share what you are reading with a broad community of readers from around the world via Facebook, Twitter, Instagram, and book-lover sites. For example, Goodreads (www.goodreads.com) allows users to track and share what they're reading and post reviews of books. On Twitter, people share the books they are currently reading with hashtags like #LoveOzYA (highlighting Australian YA books and authors) and #IMWAYR (It's Monday! What are you reading?). You can also follow book blogs and library websites to remain abreast of new publications as well as emerging writers. These ways of discovering new books, authors, and ideas are also ones you can teach to your learners.

A significant benefit of interacting with a digital community of readers worldwide is that the books' authors will occasionally join the conversation. Sometimes, prompting an author to join in is as simple as tagging the author's Twitter handle when sharing a photo, personal response, or reflection. Of course, you cannot expect authors to do this, but it is very cool when they do. Teachers and students alike also have opportunities to reach out to authors for more formal interactions, such as campus visits or digital video conferences. Local libraries and independent bookstores are good resources to find local authors who might be willing to talk to teachers and students about their writing lives. Interacting with published writers is a great way to empower emerging writers—both teachers and students—to believe that they, too, have something valuable to write and share. Incidentally, this is another compelling argument for reading contemporary literature rather than only classics—the authors are more likely to still be alive.

Now, let's talk about teachers as writers. Sometimes, when we are leading professional development sessions, we conduct a rudimentary poll, asking secondary literacy teachers about their literacy lives. Typically, when we ask, "How many of you are readers? How many of you have shared the book you are currently reading with friends?," many teachers confidently raise their hands and even share book recommendations with us. However, when we ask, "How many of you are writers? When did you last share your own personal writing with friends, colleagues, or anyone?," the majority squirm a bit, look around the room, and remain silent. We know—and the teachers we've worked with agree—it is much easier to identify as a reader, connect with titles and authors, and find beauty in what one reads. It is much, much more challenging to be a writer—to feel vulnerable and exposed, to find time for the hard work of writing well, to be critical of one's own writing, and to share it despite fear of what others may think of it.

If you are not already a writer, you may be thinking, "What do I write about?" Well, that's up to you. What's filling your heart today? Or what's weighing you down? Maybe you want to explore that. What are you wondering about? Maybe make a list of your top-ten wonderings, and see where the ideas wander. Maybe think about your best (or worst) moment in the classroom. Write just one page describing that moment, detailing the who, what, where, when, and why. There are no right or wrong topics. There's only you practicing your writing skills as any other writer does when he or she sits down to write.

When teachers reinvest in their personal reading lives and identities, they regain the love of reading and grow in their knowledge of books, genres, and authors that students will want to read as well. When teachers reinvest in their personal writing lives and identities, they regain the love of writing and grow in their knowledge of craft, style, and organization that students will want to employ as well. Teachers who invest in reading and writing influence and motivate student readers and writers to do the same in relevant and meaningful ways. These renewed reading and writing habits grow teachers' capacities as readers and writers, leading them to be better equipped to help students grow in their capacities.

Amy's Reflections From the Field

During the same summer I attended my summer institute with the National Writing Project at the University of North Texas, I attended my first of what would be many professional learning sessions with Penny Kittle at my local region center. I'd just experienced three weeks of real and personal authentic writing in a setting with peers—teachers from a wide variety of experiences and grade levels—who grew to trust one another and gave honest feedback. They pushed me as a thinker, writer, researcher, and educator. I knew I could be a better teacher.

Penny opened her session by asking participants to watch a video of spoken-word poet Shane Koyczan performing his poem "Beethoven" (McMurry, 2007) and then write in reaction to it. She said to listen carefully and then write a response to a line that spoke to us. In the poem, Koyczan repeats the phrase "not good enough," and this line resonated with me. I don't remember what I wrote. I do remember the feeling of putting my pen to the page and pouring out my thoughts, and I especially remember the trepidation I felt reading what I wrote to my colleagues who sat around my table. I didn't know these people well—we'd only worked together for a short time—but they listened, and they all took turns sharing, equally nervous. Our responses to that poem were heartfelt and fascinating, everyone selecting a different line with different significance, depending on the person and his or her own line of thinking. We bonded, maybe in the tiniest measure, in ways we hadn't previously.

continued ▶

At the end of Penny's training, as we gathered our things to leave, one of my colleagues quipped, "I remember now why I wanted to teach English. I want to read and write and share like that with my students." That's exactly how I felt. I'd experienced powerful and personal connections in that session with Penny and in the National Writing Project institute that summer, and I knew those were the experiences I wanted to create for my students. I had one spoken-word poem in my pocket I knew would get me started, and I began a journey to collect more—more meaningful texts that not only showed the beauty of language but also spoke to the soul.

Penny's book *Write Beside Them: Risk, Voice, and Clarity in High School Writing* (Kittle, 2008) became my guide as I shifted my thinking. I planned differently. I wrote beside my students. I read more and a wider variety of texts. I learned as I went. And I often felt like a failure. But then I'd ask my students to write a reflection on their learning, and they'd show me otherwise. Student after student told me that because of my class, they came to believe in themselves as writers, they read more than they ever had in the past—some finishing their first complete novel—and they understood more fully how language works and why the choices they make as writers matter.

Modeling Expert Reading and Writing Habits

Authentic literacy teachers routinely model literacy skills for their students by sharing. Teacher clarity—carefully and explicitly stating learning goals and objectives and including success criteria—makes a significant impact on student learning (Fisher et al., 2016). Teachers set success criteria by modeling reading and writing habits for learners every day—for instance, conducting book talks in which they spotlight books students may want to read, using excerpts from their personal reading or books students are reading to teach literacy skills, and promoting metacognition by thinking out loud in front of students.

Modeling the authentic habits of readers can be as simple as talking about the books you've read, those you've tried and abandoned, and those you want to read. Share with students when you've finished a book and what meaning and ideas you've taken away from it. Talk through your thoughts about the narrator (Did you like the narrator?), the plot (Did you think the conflict and resolution were realistic?), the characters (How did the writer make the characters believable?), or your overall impressions (Would you recommend this book to a friend?). We use the language of our content to authentically share our thoughts and feelings about the books we read. We call this version of modeling *book talks* (Kittle, 2013).

Modeling can also be more specific to a skill you are working on in class. For example, say your students are working on sentence combining in order to write with more variety in their sentence structure. You might model your thinking as you read your novel—how you noticed the author varies the syntax and what that does to help you as the reader. Maybe the syntax sparked an emotion that helped you relate to a character or the conflict he or she faced. You might even project a page from your book for the class to see and follow along. These things show students the success criteria for becoming a reader who notices an author's craft and clarify what you expect students to learn to do as they take on this identity. Literacy teachers model through their actions and talk that books hold value—books help people become more empathetic, and they influence them as writers.

Of course, teachers model their thinking as they write, too. Writing with students is often a sticking point with teacher writers; they are afraid to "mess up." Remember this: you can't mess up. Writing is messy. It's supposed to be hard. Ask any published writer. During lessons and in-class writing time, write with your learners, modeling the thinking and choosing of language writers do as they craft meaning. For example, say students are writing college application essays, but they are having difficulty narrowing their focus and writing with precise and significant meaning. You might show them how you're struggling similarly and ask them for help in determining a single point in your essay that you can magnify to make your essay more powerful. Or perhaps your students are writing argumentative essays but struggling with writing powerful position statements. You can show them examples of three position statements you've written for your own position paper and ask them to help you determine which packs the most punch. Or perhaps your students are practicing using imagery in their writing. You can project your writing on the board and let them point out lines that would benefit from comparisons or other image-evoking word choices. Through these exercises, you model how writers think through the choices they make, and you provide examples of how students can write and strengthen their own craft. You set the standard for success criteria, dependent on the skills intended for the writing task, as you do so.

As part of modeling expert writing, teachers can also demonstrate how writers discover topics about which they want to write. This is a point where writing and reading intersect—students' choices of books to read might indicate the topics that interest them enough to write about and students must know about their topics before they can write about them. Books are chosen perhaps because they reflect the lived experiences of the learners in the classroom. Just as English teachers often enter the profession driven by a personal love for favorite titles and authors, which most likely resonate with their personal ethnocultural experience, there are authors and titles that learners will have a significantly better chance of connecting with due to ethnocultural factors. When teachers invite learners to explore instructional texts that expose them to cultural, racial, and linguistic perspectives they can recognize and relate to, they support learning critical interpretive skills (Skerrett & Warrington, 2018). And when you model your thinking through the texts that resonate with you, students learn how to think through the texts that resonate with them.

Authentic literacy teachers know and model why writers write: for themselves because it aids personal understanding, for others because it can advocate and argue and explain in ways oral language doesn't. You are a writer, who writes for authentic audiences (Graham, 2018)—the most authentic audience being the learners in your classroom. In turn, students should write for authentic audiences as well. The most readily available audience? Their peers within the classroom community. Teacher modeling is how to transform learning communities so they become infused with student—and teacher—writers.

Instructing Individual Readers and Writers, Rather Than Teaching Prescriptive Texts and Topics

To create a shift in thinking and practice, authentic literacy teachers acknowledge the individual talents, skills, and needs of each learner in the classroom (Doghonadze & Kerdikoshvili, 2012). Just as teachers have their own personal and literacy histories, every secondary student comes to school with a history as a human and as a reader and a writer. The goal is not just to teach students literacy skills; it is to tap into the students' histories and help every learner *become* authentically literate (P. Johnston, 2004). Authentic literacy instruction requires vulnerability and risk taking. There isn't a script. There's only your personal experience and expertise, and your students' lived experience and the history of literacy they carry in their minds from the moment they walk in the door.

Regularly devote time to talk to your learners and invite them to talk to one another, like readers talk to other readers and writers talk to other writers; this will transform the classroom community and make learning dynamic, social, and motivated by the personal investment of each reader, writer, and communicator in the room. In addition, regularly meet with your readers and writers in one-on-one conferences to assess needs, teach specific skills, and validate each learner as a unique and capable individual. Remember, authentic literacy instruction means being responsive to your students' lives, getting to know your students as individuals with literacy strengths and weaknesses, and opening time and space for your students to make choices about their learning. Agency is a prerequisite for authenticity. Students choose books they want to read and make choices about the purposes, topics, and forms of their writing. As students develop their decision-making capacity, teachers guide them into making more complex choices.

All these things require teachers to tap into their students' intrinsic motivation, which propels authentic engagement in their learning. There is no one-size-fits-all literacy instruction simply because students' talents, skills, wants, and needs come in so many varying sizes. Maintaining an honest, vulnerable, student-driven, relationship-building classroom on an ongoing basis is hard work, but it's worthy work that every learner deserves. And throughout the remainder of this book, we will continue to illustrate how you can be a change agent who fills the gap between research and practice.

Summary

In the real world (and in books or in movies), people tend to dislike a person who preaches one thing and does another. You might even feel a bit of resentment toward this person and rebel against his or her example. On the other hand, people tend to cheer on the person who strives to live up to his or her ideals—even if he or she falters from time to time. It's easy to trust the person who makes you feel as if he or she understands you and then demonstrates it in his or her actions.

Given that many English teachers may have lost their love of reading, we hope this chapter inspires you to want to explore more books, be they biographies, novels, or books by basketball players or about dancing. As you immerse yourself in the world of books, especially books your students will want to read, you will see how you can use these books to make connections with your learners and build relationships and community with them. Students may not like the books you like, and that is fine. When you identify as a reader and share your reading experiences, you set success criteria and help students develop the habits of mind of authentic readers. In turn, given that the majority of teachers may not be accomplished writers, we hope you can see how taking on the challenge of becoming a writer (or a better one) as you write beside your students will inspire them—especially as you show them the messiness of your craft. They may chuckle or even mock, but in the end they will see themselves in your journey, and their cheer and wish for you to succeed will become a cheer and wish for themselves to do likewise. This is empathy in the authentic literacy classroom—the regular effort to risk being vulnerable and transparent to what students already know, which is that even the teacher can learn and get better. As you develop your authentic literacy expertise, show your students the getting better part of your journey, and they will take the risk to follow you. In the next chapter, we explore the importance of community.

Your Turn: Chapter 2

Reflecting on what you've learned in this chapter, record your primary action steps. As an authentic literacy teacher, I will:

-
-

Award-winning journalist and beloved writing teacher and mentor Donald Murray (1982) wrote this about becoming a writer:

> It is the larger responsibility of the writer to be irresponsible, to play with the truths of his or her life, to put together what doesn't seem to belong together, to make connections which sever previous connections, to use language in ways that language can't seem to be used so that the act of writing will lead the writer to unexpected meanings. (pp. 44–45)

Consider your own experiences in regard to writing. Then, choose one of the following questions, and write a response. Share your writing with a colleague, a peer, or your students.

- Describe your reading and writing life in the way Murray calls "irresponsible."
- What is the last book you read where you noticed the writer's ability to play with language in the way Murray describes? How did that writing make you feel?
- What is the last piece of writing you did that you were proud of? What was it about? Whom did you share this writing with? How did you feel while sharing it?

CHAPTER 3

Relationships and Community in the Authentic Literacy Classroom

Students' personal and social identities must matter in the classroom if secondary teachers are going to help their students learn at high levels. Each of their students is a teenager, friend, family member, learner, thinker, reader, and writer, and takes on many other identities outside of school. To instruct these individuals and respond to their lived experiences, educators must get to know them. Literacy teachers especially need to know what students believe about their abilities and capabilities as they relate to reading and writing and how students see themselves as readers and writers. In his book *Choice Words: How Our Language Affects Children's Learning*, Peter Johnston (2004) explains that students "narrate their lives, identifying themselves and the circumstances, acting and explaining events in ways they see as consistent with the person they take themselves to be" (p. 23). For secondary learners, these beliefs have formed over many prior years of schooling. If teachers don't take the time to find out how their students see themselves, they miss out on the opportunity to teach responsively to students' beliefs about who they are *and* how they learn. These student beliefs become the base on which teachers begin building authentic relationships, a key factor in authentic literacy learning.

In this chapter, you will discover the importance of building an engaging and motivating classroom community, as well as several strategies for doing so.

Amy's Reflections From the Field

I already knew they were hard workers. This group of girls spent a lot of time in my classroom after school. They huddled together at the far table, speaking in a language I did not understand. They asked questions occasionally, afraid of being wrong.

"Is this right?" one would say, timidly showing me her iPad where she'd written a few sentences in the Docs app. Returning to her table, she'd share my response with her friends. In class we watched the documentary *A Place to Stand*, based on the book by the same name

continued ▶

by Jimmy Santiago Baca (2001) who became a poet while serving time in prison. Baca's story captivated my students. They identified and analyzed the argument: "Education matters. Fight for it. Words matter. Learn them. Write them. They empower you." Some students understood that more than others. These girls, for sure.

We read several of Baca's poems. Through poetry my students more easily grasped the beauty and intention in an author's craft than reading prose. The task was for students to reread Baca's poem "As Life Was Five" and to write a reflective piece in response to it. These girls were struggling, so I finally joined them at their table.

"Tell me what's going on," I said.

"We just aren't sure," Biak said. She spoke more often than the others, although her English was only a little better.

"Can I see what you've written?" I asked, and she timidly passed me her writing, carefully penned on notebook paper.

She quickly broke into explanation: "I wanted to write my own poem. I don't know how, and I don't know . . ." Words tumbled out, and she lowered her head, waiting for me to read the page.

I looked, and before I could really read anything, the words "Burmese!! STUPID and CRAZY!" jumped out at me.

"Wait," I said, "I thought *you* were from Burma."

Five voices rose in chorus: "Yes, yes, we are from Burma, but we are not Burmese. We are Chin."

I needed them to teach me. I'd never heard of Chin, and my knowledge of Burma was limited to the first few chapters of *Saving Fish From Drowning* by Amy Tan (2005), which I'd tried to read and abandoned years ago.

"Will you tell me your story?" I asked, looking closely into the faces of these beautiful young women, similar yet so different in features and personality.

Kimi began to talk.

"We are from the state of Chin in Burma. The Chin are the mountain people. The Christians. The Burmese hate the Christians."

And then they all told me their story: These students fled Burma with their families, leaving grandparents and loved ones behind. Sometimes not getting to say goodbye for fear the secret of their journey would be told. They traveled in groups, mostly at night, "walking, walking, walking," they said. Often barely eating food, and even then, mostly rice balls or an egg stirred into water. "I lost my shoes," Biak said. "I walked for miles and miles with no shoes, and the . . . what are those things?" she turned to her friends, motioning with her hands like claws. "Those things that stuck to my feets?"

"Thorns," they said.

"Yes, thorns stuck in my feets, but I had to walk. Walk and walk."

"Walk quickly and don't let go," Kimi said.

"There was a pregnant woman with us. She could not keep up. When we reached the border of Malaysia, she could not run. I do not know what happened to her."

"I remember we heard the *pow pow pow*. We had to run as fast as we can to cross the border. I was so little. My legs short. I was so scared."

Biak began to cry. She bowed her head and covered her face with her hands. "I don't like to think about it. I remember my grandmother's face. We barely got to tell goodbye. She cried so much."

I looked around the table. Their eyes shone with memories.

"You all left family behind, didn't you?"

They nodded, and I saw a few pairs of eyes pool with tears.

"Did you travel together?"

"No! But we all have same stories. All Chin students do," Kimi said.

"Wow," I said. "Just wow." My heart beat heavy with the weight of these stories. Resilience took on new meaning.

"So you must think it's pretty lame when your classmates whine about having to work a three-hour shift and that's the reason they cannot do their homework."

The tension broke, and they laughed.

"What an amazing gift you've given me," I said. "You need to write your stories."

"I wanted to write a book," Kimi said, "but I don't know how."

I smiled. "We can work on that."

My heart—and my intentions—changed after that chat. I also felt chagrin. I had waited three months into the school year to extend the important invitation: "Tell me your story."

Those young women from the Chin state in Burma grew to trust me because I prompted, and I listened. They told me later that I was the first teacher who asked them to tell me their stories—they had all attended U.S. public schools for at least four years.

I am sure other teachers assumed they knew. I thought I knew until I saw the emotion in five pairs of eyes. "We all have same stories," Kimi had said, but that is not true. They all have similar experiences. Their stories are uniquely personal, and they serve as cardinal prerequisites to the identities of each individual. Identity matters, especially when working with adolescents. The most important conversation is the one that invites students to tell their stories.

Source: Adapted from Rasmussen (2016). Used with permission.

Instruction Based on Relationships

"Positive, humane, growth-producing teacher-student relationships" are a minimum requirement for quality instruction (Fisher et al., 2016, p. 146). At face value, this point is obvious, and few would argue with it. However, we wonder how often these relationships are truly enacted in classrooms. Often, teachers simply say relationships are important, complete a get-to-know-you activity during the first week of school, and then move on to assigning and assessing the mandatory texts and tasks. To move beyond this bare minimum, consider the significance of the word *humane* in Fisher and colleagues' (2016) description. What makes a relationship humane? Humane relationships do the following.

- Seek to understand rather than demand
- Seek to promote rather than obstruct

- Build community in ongoing and sustaining ways
- Respond to needs intentionally
- Adapt as necessary
- Benefit all parties mutually
- Produce growth

The bottom line is humane relationships are not just about the individual; they are about the whole—the community. In an authentic literacy classroom, humane relationships act as synapses, diffusing the neurotransmissions between equal participants who value the shared responsibility of thinking, reading, and writing. These relationships are often imperfect, yet irreplaceable.

Adolescents crave humane relationships and a place to belong. Teachers do too. In our experience, when students feel validated and seen, and know their voices are heard, they more willingly step into the personal and vulnerable spaces vital for critical thinking, self-expression, and self-reflection—all necessary processes for navigating relationships in school and beyond it. It is through teacher-student, student-student, and whole-class relationships that educators build classroom communities with high expectations for all learners, a prerequisite for literacy and student achievement (Fisher et al., 2016). To imagine the possibilities for your own classroom, see "Envisioning Authentic Literacy Learning Communities."

Reader Reflection: *Envisioning Authentic Literacy Learning Communities*

Knowing that the goal of a literacy class is for students to practice and develop reading, writing, listening, and speaking skills, explain what you believe constitutes the daily activity within a "positive, humane, growth-producing" community of literacy learners (Fisher et al., 2016, p. 146).

What are the students doing and saying?	What is the teacher doing and saying?

Visit ***go.SolutionTree.com/literacy*** *for a free reproducible version of this reflection.*

Active and authentic learning communities require action and authenticity. Both require language that builds trusting relationships. So how do you build a community with humane, growth-producing relationships in an authentic literacy classroom? The first step is to organize the classroom around student engagement and motivation.

Engagement-Driven Classrooms

Engagement ties directly to a student's personal investment in his or her work, and this investment rests squarely on his or her interests, ideas, and desires—and the opportunity to collaborate with peers. Adolescents are social by nature. Teachers must allow them to be social. When the instructional framework offers students opportunities to collaborate—and talk—as they learn, the class begins to move into an engagement model, rather than a compliance-based one (Pearson & Lopez, 2018).

Student engagement works differently than compliance. Engagement powers learning by empowering the learner; compliance often stymies both. A compliance-driven classroom leads to all students' doing the exact same work, and when not listening to the teacher, students work only in isolation, instead of in community (Kohn, 1999). We grew up in compliance-driven classrooms—perhaps you did too—directed by our English teachers to:

- Sit in *this* seat
- Ask and answer questions like *this*
- Read *these* important books
- Know *these* important details
- Interpret the text *this* way
- Complete *this* worksheet
- Conform writing to *this* formula
- Follow *these* writing rules
- Think *this* about *that* topic

When students dutifully complied with such directions, they might have appeared engaged. This was us. As young people in compliance-driven English classes, we dutifully complied. We followed directions, read assigned texts, completed formulaic essays, and regurgitated our teachers' lectures to pass tests. We were students doing the same thing as everyone else, and when not listening to the teacher, we worked in silence at our desks, instead of in community (Kohn, 1999). At the time, we didn't know the difference between compliance and engagement. We didn't know that when teachers truly engage their learners, it can make *all* the difference.

Amy once saw a poster in a classroom that stated, "If you are talking, you are not learning." That is the antithesis of what 21st century learners need. They need lots of talk—about what they read and what they write and what they think about reading and writing *and* what they think about their lives—especially if we hope they will write from their lives, the seedbed of all authentic ideas. Of course, we understand that no teacher likes to have students talking when he or she is providing direct instruction. But engagement-driven classrooms use far less teacher-centered and lecture-based instruction, creating time for students to learn through conversation, collaboration, and active reading and writing.

Engagement begins with the idea that we meet learners where they are (and who they are)—instead of where (or who) we expect them to be. A compliance-focused classroom purports to teach learners *what* to think, read, write, and communicate; an engagement-driven authentic literacy classroom endeavors to teach learners *how* to think, read, write, and communicate. *How to think* is the edge when it comes to engagement.

True Motivations

Engagement and community in an authentic literacy classroom include seeking to understand students' true motivations for all things literacy. Teachers must assess barriers students may have built around English class: Do they like to read? Why or why not? Do they enjoy writing? Why or why not? As you begin to learn how your students feel about ELA and why they might be motivated (or not) to participate, you will become more adept at engaging them in authentic literacy habits, which will lead to lowering their self-imposed barriers. It's these barriers—sometimes called *fears*—that most often restrict students from fully participating in a learning community where individual ideas, interests, and passions drive instruction. Quite simply, students might be afraid to tell you what they think. Therefore, developing relationships that empower students (Pearson & Lopez, 2018) is an essential element of authentic literacy learning and instruction.

In 1983, educator and writing expert Donald Graves wrote *Writing: Teachers and Children at Work*, a book that presented revolutionary ideas about writing instruction. In the first few paragraphs, he points out that children, at a very young age, come to school wanting to write. Most parents would agree with this observation, perhaps reflecting on the crayon- and marker-inscribed walls at home. Graves explains that those marks are students' proclaiming, "I am." Yet the traditional approach to literacy education tragically replies to those hopeful young writers, "No, you aren't" (Graves, 1983, p. 3). Instead of embracing young people's identities and engaging them in writing about who they are and what they know, teachers too often deny young writers the chance to share the very things that make them who they are.

If teachers fail to extract, validate, and leverage *who* students are, then they fail to understand how relationships work. And knowing who students are takes more time than the first few days of school. It requires ongoing discovery (for the teacher and each student) throughout the entire school year as texts and writing tasks reflect, reveal, and form who each student is—and who he or she can become (Pearson & Lopez, 2018). Community is the result of teacher-student relationships, built on finding out individual interests, motivations, histories, and goals; plus, student-student relationships develop through the sharing of individual interests, motivations, histories, and goals. Knowing your students' identities is imperative to effective teaching—especially the teaching of authentic literacy. This knowledge ignites the relationships students need to feel safe. It's here you have the chance to establish patterns for authentic lifelong reading and writing.

To authentically engage students, you need to know who they are and thus what interests and motivates them to learn. In other words, you must learn what is relevant and meaningful to their lives (Skerrett & Warrington, 2018). Often, the events currently happening in their communities, states or provinces, and nations are the most relevant. While many adolescents admittedly do not pay attention to the news, the language surrounding the issues that students personally experience abounds in opportunities to teach relevant skills. Using current events in literacy education can help teachers meet the goal of teaching critical-thinking skills as they relate to language. Plus, if students are to leave secondary school prepared for the challenges of adulthood, ready to engage in civic life and discourse, it is wise to practice the literacy skills needed to do so, such as identifying bias, determining tone, understanding nuance, supporting an argument, verifying facts, validating sources, and researching beyond the first hits on Google. We know high school English is not a civics course, but that doesn't mean ELA teachers cannot use texts and themes that correspond with those taught in civics as they teach ELA skills. There's freedom in ELA to choose texts on topics that are personally relevant and meaningful to the lives of students. You fast-track motivation and come to know your students more personally when you capitalize on that and use texts that are already relevant to the students you teach instead of needing to make them relevant.

Constructing a community built on authentic relationships, engagement, and motivations creates space to challenge students' thinking, ideas, and beliefs about themselves as learners—*and* the world in which they live. Without authentic relationships, how can teachers hope to equip students to engage with and improve the world? When they become adults, these same students will stand beside you in line to vote, become your neighbors (if they aren't already), hold key positions in your communities, and maybe even hire you for jobs. Without humane, authentic relationships, we don't think authentic learning is possible, but with them, you generate a great deal of hope, for yourself and your students. See "Learning About Your Students" to reflect on the boundless potential of these relationships.

Reader Reflection: *Learning About Your Students*

"What should I know about you?"

Imagine asking your students to respond to this question on the first day of class—or at least within the first week of school. Then, in response, you communicate either in writing or verbally some kind of acknowledgment of what they tell you.

How might doing this questioning and responding empower students and potentially give you important insights into their interests and motivations, as well as their strengths and struggles as literacy learners?

Visit ***go.SolutionTree.com/literacy*** *for a free reproducible version of this reflection.*

Some of the Ways Authentic Literacy Teachers Build Relationships and Create Communities

Real relationships are hard work. They take time. They take effort and intentionality. Humans in general hesitate to be vulnerable with each other, but vulnerability can often make a relationship—or break it, without the necessary trust. So teachers have to create trusting environments where all learners feel safe and seen (Fisher et al., 2016) and where they want to freely share their ideas and opinions. To do the work of authentic literacy, students need to be willing to take risks and share their identities through talking, reading, writing, and collaborating within a community.

An authentic literacy teacher takes the following actions.

- Welcomes students to the classroom and fosters each student's personal identity
- Shares his or her own identity with students, including interests, strengths, challenges, goals, and so on, and invites students to share their own
- Gathers information about his or her students to get to know them as individual learners and design responsive instruction
- Invites students to share their personal reactions to texts

We explore each action in the following sections and provide space for you to record your primary action steps in the "Your Turn" reproducible at the end of the chapter (page 50).

Welcoming Students and Fostering Their Identities

Think of the first day of school. So often on this day, secondary teachers assign seats, pass out a syllabus, outline class rules, and tell students the expectations for the course. We used to do this too. Now, we think it is possibly the worst way to start the school year, especially for so many adolescents who do not want to be at school in the first place. Even well-intentioned teachers ignite negative emotions on the first day instead of warm and welcoming ones. Think about it: Do students' initial encounters with the teacher in the classroom make the students want to stay, flee, or put their heads on their desks and ignore the world around them? Allowing students to choose their seats and keeping teacher monologues about class rules, dry syllabi, expectations, and grading policies to a minimum declaratively tells all students, "You matter more than I do. Stay."

A positive, welcoming, safe environment is a literacy expert's top priority. To launch the school year by systematically building an inviting classroom, we suggest the following.

- Beginning on day one, greet students individually and try to notice something personal about them. Ideally, at-the-door greetings are best, but any genuine greeting lets learners know you see them. Continue this action every day, or as often as possible, throughout the school year.
- Allow students to sit where they are comfortable. Let them sit near their friends, especially on the first day of school. Then, let them stay in their chosen seats throughout the course—as long as they respect the learning community you invite them to build with you.

- Learn students' names and how to pronounce them correctly, validating cultures and ethnicities. Names are a valuable part of each person's identity. Take the time to listen to how students pronounce their names. In our experience, many students will not correct an adult when their name is mispronounced. You must do the hard work of getting students' names right, and the quicker you learn everyone's name, the better for your community. Be sure you also help students know the names of the peers they will spend class time with. Depending on the size of your school and students' class sizes, learning everyone's name can be a rewarding challenge.
- Consider not presenting the syllabus on day one; instead, share your personal goals as a reader and writer, and invite students to think of their own. Be creative and have fun. Students will appreciate your enthusiasm for your subject as they see you authentically enjoy reading and writing, and this is your first opportunity to build credibility as a learner as well as a teacher.
- Within the first week or so of school, share personal interests, perhaps introducing yourself through video, images, stories, or favorite quotes or snippets of poetry. These interests might include your family, hobbies, education, goals, or anything you, in turn, want to learn about your students. As you share your interests, explain how these things have shaped your identity, especially your identity as a reader and writer. Then, consider asking students to craft a similar product as a way to introduce themselves to you and their peers. This activity can serve as a genesis of sorts as you work to magnify all student voices, recognize their unique talents and interests, and create a safe space for your learners.

The resulting classroom community then brings students back again and again. And not just back into the classroom, but back into a space where they want to learn. The key to community building is balancing sense of self and sense of others. In short, self and community go hand in hand. And in like measure, in an authentic literacy classroom, community and curriculum require a similar balance. To maintain a community where students have agency, students drive the curriculum, which means literacy teachers need viable curricula that allow time and space for welcoming students, building relationships, and establishing community. Remember, students' lived experiences, cultures, backgrounds, interests, and wants—and maybe even the goals they have for themselves and their futures—are the content that supports literacy skills. Learning about their needs as individuals starts the moment young people walk in the classroom door—so they will stay.

Figure 3.1 (page 46) illustrates how including students' interests in the curriculum both improves learning and builds community.

Sharing Interests, Strengths, Challenges, and Goals

A community of readers and writers starts with the teacher—the most adept reader and writer in the room. He or she sets the expectation for an authentic, relationship-rich community by sharing his or her identity with the class: his or her interests, hopes and dreams, strengths and challenges, and personal goals. Most important, an authentic literacy teacher,

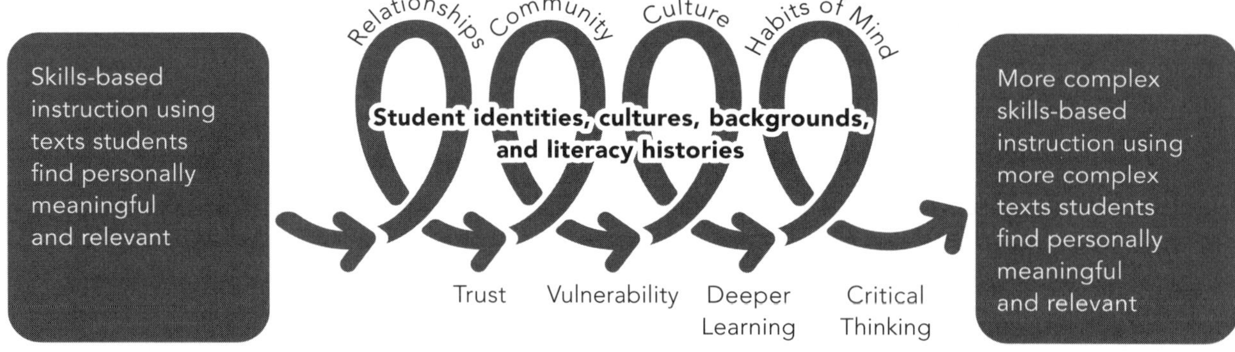

Figure 3.1: The interconnectivity and reciprocal nature of authentic literacy instruction.

intent on building credibility along with growing in expertise, tells short personal stories, related to life and literacy learning (using humor when possible to lower stress levels and invite engagement), and writes daily beside students, all the while sharing his or her personal writing. Through this modeling, the teacher sets an expectation for the way a community of writers builds relationships by sharing and eliciting feedback. He or she models how this process influences the types of meaningful stories a writer produces to engage an audience, and he or she demonstrates the ways a writer builds relationships with other writers—drawing on others' skills and expertise to develop his or her own—all the while building a personal reading and writing legacy.

Gathering Information About Students

An authentic literacy expert gathers as much data as he or she can about his or her students. Consider the following approaches to information gathering.

- **Distribute and analyze student interest surveys:** These can be as simple or complex as you deem necessary, depending on your individual students. While interest surveys can look like worksheets, you may want to avoid those due to their lack of authenticity. Think of interest surveys more like simple party games. Sometimes a simple survey question can bring humor into the room—and also give you bonus information about students' literacy skills. For example, asking students to write down their favorite movie along with a microsummary told from the point of view of the protagonist or the conflict personified can tell you what genres students like, and the way they write the response can tell you if they understand the basics of writing a summary. As another option, asking students to make a list of three to five activities that they enjoy outside of school, using descriptive or figurative language in each bullet, gives you information about how they spend their time, and it tells you if your writers can use imaginative word choice.
- **Listen in on student conversations:** When you ask students to complete even the simplest of surveys, you will also ask them to read aloud what they write to at least one peer. This sets the expectation that students will share their writing, and it affords you the opportunity to listen in—yes, as a way

to monitor conversations, but most important, as a way to learn about your students. Most adolescent learners cannot help adding commentary to what they or their peers write. This commentary can inform how you might plan next steps, determine what your students think about a topic, learn about how your students feel about themselves as readers and writers, and glean an abundance of other valuable information you can use as a responsive and authentic literacy teacher.

- **Ask students to complete baseline writing tasks:** The last thing you want students to do is feel bored with the first writing task you give them. Having students write to a narrow prompt is a surefire way to ruin your initial attempts at developing positive relationships and quickly growing a community of readers and writers. However, asking students to complete baseline writing tasks can give you important information about your students' lives and about their abilities as readers and writers. You just have to give students options and invite them to tap into topics they already know about. For example, perhaps one objective your students must be able to accomplish is writing an informational essay, so you want to give them a baseline writing task that helps you determine what they know about informational writing. Let students choose topics they know and care about—athletic shoes, sports teams, band instruments, fast-food restaurants, hair products, mowing the lawn, sibling rivalry, cafeteria food, digital learning, and so on. If your intent is to see how well your students can write an informational essay, they do not need a prompt. The same holds true for any form of baseline writing, be it personal narrative or persuasive essay. Students need the freedom to show what they can do with a topic they might actually be interested in. And later, when you read their writing, you'll get a glimpse into their lives, personally and academically. And these glimpses will help you know how to teach them.
- **Talk individually with students about their likes and dislikes:** As mentioned previously, talk is a vital function in an authentic literacy classroom. When you engage in conversation with your students, you even the playing field. Talking with students about seemingly mundane or extremely complex likes and dislikes can be a powerful equalizer. Now, you may think you are too busy or too awkward or too afraid to say something wrong. Guess what? So are your students. And when you talk to them like the young adults they are, you come to know them individually, so you can teach them in the unique ways they deserve.

Collecting as much information as possible about who students are as individuals and how they integrate as a community is a valuable use of instructional time. It allows you to be responsive to learners' needs as early and often as possible. Get students talking. The culture in an authentic literacy classroom is a culture of reciprocity.

Billy's Reflections From the Field

When I first joined my school district as a leader for secondary literacy classrooms, I was charged with implementing authentic literacy practices in high school English classrooms. While I was excited at this direction, I was also somewhat surprised at the intensive mindset of district leaders toward this goal. It's not that I disagreed with moving toward a more student-centered approach in high school language arts; in fact, I was thrilled with the prospect! But I wondered if leadership understood exactly how much change we would be asking of our teachers. My outward response was "That's incredible! I can't wait to get started!" What I really wanted to ask was "Are you sure you know what this means?"

By a few years into the implementation, district leadership knew what it meant. It meant transforming our words into actions by investing in developing teacher expertise through multi-week summer institutes, which built community districtwide and in teacher teams on campuses; investing in classroom libraries for every high school classroom, and reading and sharing these books in communities so individual teachers felt prepared to share them with student readers; and investing in timely discussions that challenged long-standing English classroom traditions, identities, nostalgia, the literary canon, and teacher-centered practices. Finally, and perhaps most important for an instructional shift of this magnitude to work, it meant investing in better communication within the community that housed our schools, so families understood why we were making sweeping instructional shifts.

While there were certainly bumps in the road, teachers and students began to thrive with an emphasis on authentic literacy practices. The anchor along the way, holding us steady through the challenges during change, was the community and the deep relationships we built.

My first year, I set a personal goal: to build such close relationships and such a tight community that, in the times of celebration and trouble, the teachers I work among would have no choice but to turn to each other.

I still have the wrinkled sticky note I wrote this goal on as a reminder.

Relationships and community are the foundation of engagement in authentic literacy practices (Pearson & Lopez, 2018). Without them, the vulnerable, risk-seeking habits and routines that are necessary for instructional shifts would not be possible. I instinctively knew this as I challenged teachers to reconsider their identities as literacy educators—challenged them to read, think, plan, and practice with a student-centered, skill-driven focus instead of a teacher-centered, text-driven one. And while the work has been difficult and provocative and intimidating at times, it has also been vastly rewarding and empowering and significant. The work has happened and continues to happen due to the power of the relationships and community that drive us back to each other, instead of against each other.

Inviting Personal Reactions

Authentic literacy teachers set a daily expectation for shared reading, thoughts, responses, and expressions, bringing in a wide variety of texts for students to experience as readers and emulate as writers. Especially at the beginning of the school year, make an effort to share texts that model the way writers share their identities and think about the identities of others around them. Encourage students to not just understand what the meaning of the text is but to notice how the author crafts it (word choice, sentence variety, figurative language, and so on; see Personal Response Writing, page 63). As you share texts for students to react to, explain the value of mentor texts (that is, texts to respond to, study, imitate, or learn from; see Mentor Texts, page XX). After modeling your own response, invite students to respond to these texts in writing, teasing out their thinking onto the page. Ask students to share their reactions to these texts in pairs or small groups while you listen to the ensuing discussions and assess your learners' thinking. All the while, you can continue to gather data related to the individual identities, strengths, and challenges making up the classroom community—data that help inform planning for future instructional opportunities. These instructional moves set the expectations that in your class the community will engage in reading various texts in different forms by a variety of authors as you read and study texts together and share what you think about them in your writing and with each other.

When considering texts you might use to generate personal reactions, consider what your students will consider thought provoking and help them think about their own identities as young humans—and as readers and writers. As a daily practice, authentic literacy teachers intentionally guide their newly formed community of learners in reading a variety of texts that invite personal reactions. For example, you could share *Artists, Writers, Thinkers, Dreamers* by James Gulliver Hancock (2014) and invite students to craft visual autobiographies that resemble the biographies featured in that book. Or, introduce *The Book of Lists* by David Wallechinsky and Amy Wallace (2005) and invite students to create lists, writing with a focus on identity. The appendix (page XX) lists a number of texts we recommend for this purpose.

Student writers share their thoughts and feelings as they write. They share what they've written, and they learn about one another as young humans with memories, experiences, and opinions—and as learners. Once you have them on board, writing volumes about things they care about in the pages of their notebooks, you can guide them into learning and practicing specific writing skills that will help them grow in their confidence and capabilities as writers.

Summary

Creating an authentic community of learners, contingent on humane relationships, opens up possibilities for the deeper learning students crave and deserve. Intentional creation of a community—one that acknowledges and leverages their individual identities and motivations—establishes the everyday intrinsic motivation learners need to engage in routines fundamental to an authentic literacy classroom. This authentic community creates a space where you and your students take time to reflect on strengths and areas for growth. This daily reflection and self-evaluation creates the seedbed for intentional learning throughout the school year.

Initially, instructional planning takes a lot of effort, but it gets easier. Think of it like priming the pump: before any water comes out—and while you are pumping like crazy to get water to come out—you have to pour a lot of precious water down the pump. But, by analogy, at some point the desired learning springs forth and perpetuates itself. Authentic, powerful learning is achievable, and investing in what is required to make it happen every day in your classroom is worth doing. This investment allows teachers and students to experience authentic literacy in full measure—and may be just what adolescent learners need. The world needs them to be capable adults who can make productive and positive decisions that make our world the kind of place where all humanity can thrive.

Your Turn: Chapter 3

Reflecting on what you've learned in this chapter, record your primary action steps. As an authentic literacy teacher, I will:

-

-

Consider this statement from the book *Gilded Cage* by Vic James (2017): "Trust was what made everything possible. Trust lent you someone else's eyes, someone else's strong arms, or quick brain. Made you bigger than just yourself. Trust was how the club worked" (p. 179). Now, think about trust in the context of relationships and community as discussed in this chapter. Choose one of the following questions and write your thinking. Then, share your writing with your own community. This might be your family, friends, colleagues, or students.

- Begin with the phrase, "Trust lends you __________," and write about how trust builds relationships with students and solidifies and sustains a learning community.

- Make a list of songs, poems, quotes, videos, excerpts from books you read, infographics, and images you could use with students to spark ideas for writing that can help you get to know your students.

- Describe an experience you've had in a community of learners where trust made "everything possible." What were the students doing? What was the teacher doing? What did the experience look like, sound like, and feel like?

CHAPTER 4

Promotion of Student Choice for Greater Outcomes

Far too often in public education, classrooms are devoid of opportunities for students to make choices related to their learning. In English classes, this is demonstrated by the long-held tradition of teachers' choosing which texts students should read, which topics they should write about, and in which genre they should write. While one might attempt to blame these traditional choices on system constraints such as mandated curricula, required standards for learning, and inevitable high-stakes tests, these habits often persist because many educators experienced them when they were learning in secondary classrooms. In fact, Richard DuFour, Rebecca DuFour, Robert Eaker, Thomas W. Many, and Mike Mattos (2016) observe, "Teachers and administrators are typically so immersed in their traditional ways of doing things that they find it difficult to step outside of those traditions to examine conventional practices from a fresh, critical perspective" (p. 22).

Many experts in the field of literacy challenge teacher-centered norms, including Gay Ivey and Douglas Fisher (2006), who write, "A one-size-fits-all approach to the curriculum does not respond to the unique needs, strengths, or interests of adolescents" (p. 2). In fact, Allison Skerrett and Amber Warrington (2018) find that "literature instruction often focuses on a single text for whole-class study" and "most literature instruction continues to privilege the Euro-Western canon" (p. 412). These traditional ELA approaches often eliminate the voices of people of color, show a limited view of oppression, or further the trope of the White savior. It is well past time to practice purposeful instruction that centers people of color in mainstream curricula. One way to do this is through teachers' purposefully selecting texts for instruction, and another is through teachers' making self-selected independent reading (see page 114) a permanent part of ELA instructional routines. The world of literature is rife with choices, and teachers have a responsibility to present a wide range of inclusive possibilities and let students choose. This chapter considers the essential nature of choices and provides practical information on teaching students to make effective literacy choices.

Billy's Reflections From the Field

The teachers I work with often tell me of their experiences as they move into authentic literacy practices. The following experience illustrates the importance of students' making choices about the books they read.

On the first day of school, Ms. Hill noticed a student, Mia, slip into a familiar reading zone—a book had hooked her. While the other students in class spent time exploring several books, trying them out—frowning, smiling, confused, interested—Ms. Hill watched Mia turning page after page, lost to the classroom around her. Shyly, at the end of class, Mia asked Ms. Hill if she could take the book home. Ms. Hill warmly assented, marveling at the immediate connection Mia made to this book while wondering what exactly it was that had sparked.

The next day, Mia walked into class and immediately began reading the book again, and Ms. Hill observed that Mia must have read last night, because she was nearly halfway through the book. Excited, Ms. Hill sat next to Mia and asked her how she liked the book so far and what really drew her to it. Quiet at first, Mia emotionally explained: this was her first time reading a book with a character who struggled with an eating disorder, just like her. She shared that last night, she had found the courage to tell her parents about her eating disorder for the first time, after struggling and hiding it for the past six years.

Mia went on to tearfully ask if she could continue to talk to Ms. Hill about this in class, as she read the book and processed it; she knew reading a book so personally relevant to her own experience would be an emotional challenge for her. After a hug, Ms. Hill explained that was one of the most important things students would do in class this year: talk, and write, and share (when ready, because writers make choices about sharing) about the issues and realities that impact their lives and the world around them.

Books and choice help people see, understand, and talk about things deep inside them that they either don't recognize or try to ignore. And, while Mia's experience may not be the norm so early in the school year—since most deep relationships take time to develop—it is the exact kind of connection we know teachers can ensure for all readers when they let them choose.

Source: Adapted from Eastman (2019). Used with permission.

Choices That Benefit Student Learning

Choice makes learning personal, real, and—need we say it?—authentic. Choice fosters intrinsic motivation, which paves the way for deep consolidation of learning: skills becoming part of a student's repertoire to the level of automaticity (Fisher et al., 2016; Hattie & Donoghue, 2016). Rather than trying to make traditional texts seem relevant to all students, authentic literacy teachers choose to include texts that are *already* relevant and timely to students' lived experiences. Not only does this save valuable time, but it empowers students with reading and writing tasks they *want* to spend time doing. Alfie Kohn (1999) contends that "intrinsic motivation is more desirable than extrinsic, and that no amount of the latter can make up for the absence of the former" (pp. 97–98). Having personally motivated and invested students is critical to some of the most significant outcomes of learning: transfer, independent application of skills, and ownership of learning (Fisher et al., 2016).

Teachers need to foster a sense of engagement in literacy with students, but motivation to be engaged occurs first (Guthrie & Wigfield, 2018). Fostering relevance through choice motivates students to be active participants in their learning environment. Figure 4.1 shows the progression that is possible when students' personal interests guide their learning.

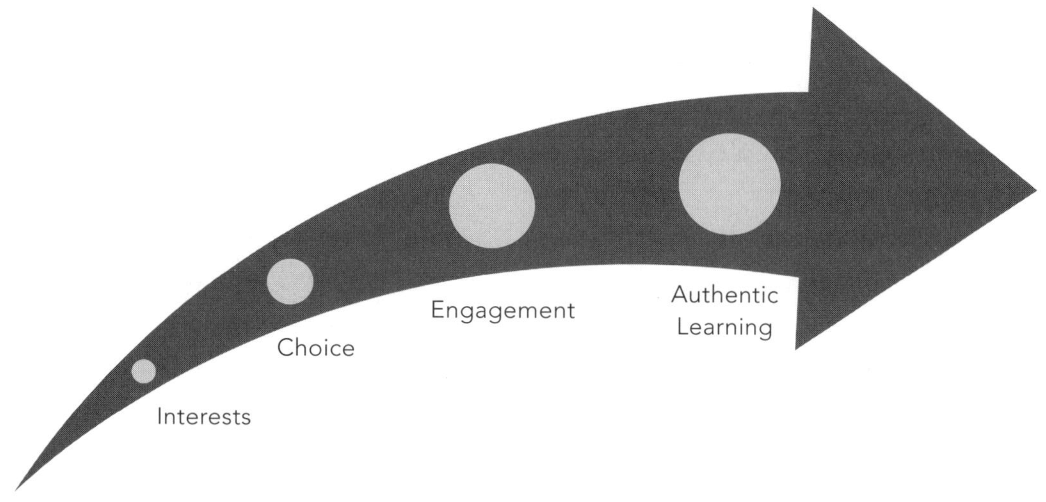

Figure 4.1: Progression from individual interests to authentic learning.

Once students' intrinsic motivation kicks in, teachers leverage it by increasingly inviting students to be the center of their learning. Teachers guide students to choose books outside their comfort zones, knowing that reading can influence how these young people view the world (Skerrett & Warrington, 2018). We believe that reading literature can be powerful, potentially helping youth develop the philosophies and characteristics of well-rounded, empathetic human beings. Teachers extend humane relationships (see page 39) beyond the classroom when they encourage students to read a wide variety of books by diverse authors with characters of diverse backgrounds, experiences, and perspectives. Now, you may be thinking, "But the books I choose for my students to read do this too." That may be true, but how many of your students actually read the books you choose? Just like anyone invested in his or her learning, secondary students want to have choices in theirs, and when it comes to books they read in ELA classes, in our experience, more students read when they choose their own. Admittedly, some students may only choose books similar to their own lived experiences, and some students will never voluntarily pick up any book with more than a hundred pages. Choice does not make things easy—for the student or for the teacher. Teachers still want students to analyze and internalize the themes of rich literature. Students still need to be willing to read literature with rich themes.

Of course, ELA classes should not just offer choices when it comes to reading. Students need to make choices as writers as well. When teachers invite students to make choices about their writing, more students willingly engage in the writing process. Authentically guiding students to ask questions and choose topics that stretch their thinking and clarify their beliefs will help some writers find catharsis and others embark on discovery during the process. Writing shifts from being something students do for school to something they do for themselves. Writing becomes purposeful when it is personal—and choice has the potential to make it so. In addition, and perhaps even most important, when student writers choose their audience—someone or some group other than the teacher—they are more apt to make purposeful choices within their writing. In fact, Linda Rief (2019) writes, literacy experts such as "Don Graves, Don Murray, Peter Elbow, Nancie Atwell, Andrea Lunsford, Janet Emig, Tom Romano, James Moffett, John Dewey, Penny Kittle, Kelly Gallagher, just to name a few, all advocate for writing for real reasons for a real audience" (p. 32). In essence, by embracing choice as part of their instructional methodology, authentic literacy teachers empower readers and writers in ways that teacher-centric instruction does not. Reflect on your starting point in this area with the questions in "Motivating and Empowering Students."

Reader Reflection: *Motivating and Empowering Students*

Knowing teachers face outside influences when it comes to instruction within their classrooms (campus or district initiatives, state- or province-mandated exams, and so on), consider the following questions based solely on the things you can control within the scope of your instruction.

How empowered do you feel your students are when it comes to their learning? Circle one of the following.

Not empowered   A little empowered   Totally empowered

How might you more effectively leverage students' intrinsic motivation through the practice of choice?

Visit ***go.SolutionTree.com/literacy*** *for a free reproducible version of this reflection.*

Some of the Ways Authentic Literacy Teachers Guide Readers and Writers in Making Choices

Here is a reality: many students struggle to make choices, even when given the opportunity. They may not know what books they would want to read because they do not have a concrete reading identity. They may not know what types of books they like, or why they do not like others. It's likely they haven't been given enough freedom in their reading lives to find out. The same holds true for writing. Students may not understand the fundamental reasons writers write, or that writing can be powerful, moving, rhythmic, or incendiary—all due to the choices writers make as they compose. Depending on how secondary students have been taught to write, they may not even know that writers make choices. Grammar, vocabulary, punctuation—these are all choices writers make when constructing meaning. It's time to stop teaching these things outside the context of authentic ideas students want to write about. Remember, the ultimate goal is to help students develop as authentic readers and writers who do the things real readers and writers do.

Creating opportunities for students to make choices and modeling how to make them is vital to authentic literacy instruction. However, it's not sufficient to simply give students access to choice. In fact, when given too many options, students may feel overwhelmed and make no choice at all. Authentic literacy teachers provide options within the scope of what students need to be engaged, learn skills, reach objectives, and show their learning. This does not mean a free-for-all or anything resembling a lack of planning. Planning for student choice is imperative, as is ensuring students have the thinking and decision-making skills to make appropriate, effective decisions.

Making effective choices requires skills—skills directly taught and modeled by an expert reader, writer, thinker, and communicator. That is you. To promote student choice in the classroom, an authentic literacy teacher does the following.

- Curates a robust classroom library so students will have many enticing books to choose from
- Teaches readers to make choices, including sharing book selection strategies and talking about books and their content and themes with students
- Teaches writers to make choices, including eliminating restrictive writing prompts, templates, and mandated graphic organizers; and using excerpts from books to teach students how writers craft meaning

As you explore these actions in the following sections, think about which ones you might try, and record your primary action steps in the "Your Turn" reproducible at the end of the chapter (page 70).

Curating Robust Classroom Libraries

Hand in hand with developing expertise as an authentic literacy teacher is ensuring the best and most authentic resources are at your and your students' fingertips. These rich resources create what John T. Guthrie and Allan Wigfield (2018) call "literature-rich classrooms" (p. 64), where students have the opportunity to read books of their choice and preference daily. A literature-rich classroom provides students with "a wealth of books [that are] immediately accessible within the classroom" (Guthrie & Wigfield, 2018, p. 64)—in short, a classroom library.

The books in a robust classroom library should be books adolescent learners want to read. Traditionally, secondary ELA classrooms have focused on classic literature: authors and texts generally accepted for their place in the canon. As you develop your classroom library, you must not merely complement the classics with current, relevant, engaging YA literature; you must purposefully put the current, relevant, engaging YA literature at the center. That's the surest way to connect with and motivate the most students to construct and maintain lifelong literacy habits.

Unfortunately, some people think of classroom libraries as only for pleasure reading, but a classroom library can be more. In authentic literacy classrooms, it *should* be more. The books students choose can serve as frontline instructional materials. A classroom library, curated as instructional materials and shared with readers, opens possibilities beyond students' reading independently for pleasure—this library provides the opportunity to leverage each student's intrinsically motivated reading habit into authentic and relevant literacy instruction.

Inclusive classroom libraries filled with vibrant, diverse, and timely literature meet students where they are as readers, writers, and thinkers, leading to student-centered learning that is authentic, relevant, and intrinsically motivating for secondary learners. What other reasons does one need to advocate for resources like this?

Unfortunately, advocate is often exactly what teachers need to do. In our experience working with hundreds of teachers in a variety of schools and districts, funding for books for secondary ELA and reading classrooms has traditionally been devoted to the aforementioned canonical literature. Even more pervasive is the expenditure of instructional-material funds on literature and grammar textbooks—the antithesis of authentic resources. Not only are textbooks outdated as soon as they are printed, but they don't meet students' need for intrinsic motivation. Inclusive, wide-ranging books written for the purpose of engaging adolescent audiences compel students to read in secondary ELA and reading classrooms, unlike most textbooks, even if those textbooks come packaged with fancy online options, ready-made quizzes, and class sets of novels. (Whole-class novel sets may have a small place in your instructional calendar, but this certainly does not justify the bulk of funds being spent on textbooks.) We envision classroom libraries filled with colorful titles and covers, award-winning and newly emerging authors, and a vast array of genres and topics. Authentic literacy teachers shun the use of instructional materials that are seen only in schools in favor of real books that real readers want to read.

A well-curated, inclusive classroom library contains a variety of classic, contemporary, traditional, and diverse texts and authors. But which ones? Teachers, parents, and commentators fiercely debate over which books students should read, particularly in secondary schools. Many educators and parents believe that students need to read the "important" books to be ready for high-stakes exams, college, and even participation in society and culture. While it is true that common perceptions of "important" books have expanded to be more contemporary and inclusive, the idea of having a list of the best books to read continues to be problematic. Who gets to decide which books are important?

A system like a canon prioritizes the past over the future, and it prioritizes individual titles and authors over the needs of individual learners. Sure, knowing about a wide variety of books from classic traditions might be valuable. It just isn't as valuable as knowing your individual learners and considering their needs. It's certainly not as valuable as students' actual ability to read. In secondary ELA classrooms, the students are literacy learners, not English majors. The moment a teacher claims *To Kill a Mockingbird* (Lee, 1960) is *the* important book all students need to read in high school, reading (and learning) becomes about the teacher and the text, rather than the student.

Instead, authentic literacy teachers invite the exploration of issues that matter to individual learners as the basis for students' selecting books they want to read. These topics might include racial inequality and the need for equitable social and judicial systems, body image, objectivity in the news and on social media, family relationships, and evaluating decisions based on one's own and others' well-being, and many more. The teacher's job, then, is to ensure readers know how to identify and analyze the significant issues in books as they relate to their lives and the world at large. This is how inquiry-based, student-centered learning works in an authentic literacy classroom: crafting intentional, strategic opportunities for thinking and exploration by knowing your students deeply and then placing the right teaching and texts in students' paths.

So how do you know which books to put in classroom libraries? Ideally, you would wait to choose the books until you get to know your students. Since this is often impractical, think about common adolescent issues, concerns, and problems, and learn about local demographics. You can use your judgment and knowledge of your school's population to get a sense of what topics and books your students might like to read. You can turn to resources like the Assembly on Literature for Adolescents (ALAN) of the National Council of Teachers of English (NCTE), the Young Adult Library Services Association (YALSA), and the International Literacy Association (ILA) and read about books you think will capture the attention, hearts, and minds of your students. You can also tap into the extensive network of literacy teachers on Twitter and other social media who share recommendations, reviews, and ways they are helping their students develop reading identities.

While we can't say that there are any books that belong in *every* secondary classroom library—the options are too vast and students too diverse—we do believe some titles are worthy of every secondary teacher's consideration. The appendix (page 137) includes a list of YA books we've found useful in helping our own students discover personal answers and explore others' conflicts as they've come to enjoy reading. Of course, we also want to guide our students to read other books besides YA, so our classroom libraries include other works of "literary merit." (Acknowledging that literary merit is subjective and not the sole qualification when it comes to developing readers, we do agree that classroom libraries must include rich texts that tackle the complexities of the human condition in complex and beautifully written ways.) The appendix also includes a list of books outside the realm of YA that we recommend.

Of course, any list of recommended books is only a snapshot of the wealth and breadth you can offer students via a robust classroom library. Poetry collections, graphic novels, novels in verse, literary nonfiction books, play scripts, and magazines are also part of what makes up a healthy, inclusive, and wide-ranging classroom library. And a classroom library is never in stasis; it organically grows, evolves, and changes as authentic literacy teachers curate it to meet the needs of the students who will use it.

To help students identify as readers, you have to help them find the desire to read. When you surround them with books they can relate to, and talk about these books and your own reading life, and share how you've found answers to personal questions within the books you read, you exemplify the value of reading as a tool for personal problem solving—an advantage real readers have that nonreaders may not. So many students swim in personal problems. Reading books that help them find answers might be their life raft.

After ensuring that students have access to books they choose to read, authentic literacy teachers ensure students have time to read them. Reading becomes a habit with practice. If independent reading is to become a lifelong part of students' identities, then teachers must devote daily class time to reading. We discuss the routine of self-selected independent reading in more detail in chapter 7 (page 114).

Amy's Reflections From the Field

When I first started teaching high school English, I thought it was all about the books. I loved literature, so I wanted students to love literature. How could they love it if I didn't help them see the complex beauty of well-crafted sentences and heartbreakingly human plotlines? I was *that* teacher: I taught books instead of readers.

Like many new teachers, I taught like I had been taught. I did not focus on the learners and their needs. I did not focus on the readers and their interests, their abilities, or anything that matters for actually growing readers. My focus sat fully on what I thought a high school English class should include: classic literature (chosen by me), study questions (written by me), analytical essays (prompted by me), and helping my students "understand" what they had just read. (I didn't even consider that my students may not have read the assigned pages at all.)

I remember the first day of my teaching career. I was teaching ninth grade. Students sat in assigned seats, alphabetically by last name. I asked all students, seat by seat, row by row, to tell everyone their name and one thing they hoped to learn in their freshman English class. I have no memory of what any of them said—except for one.

"My name is K.C., and I hate White people."

I am a White woman.

I might have felt stunned, hurt, appalled. I do remember thinking, "The audacity!," and internally huffing. I tried not to let those words sink me before I ever got afloat, and for the most part, I think I succeeded. K.C. and I learned to work together that year, and she did fine in my class. She read the books I assigned (not really). She wrote the essays (kind of).

But my idea of success is much different now than it was back then; I no longer think fine is ever good enough.

If I could relive day one of my first year teaching and my interaction with K.C., I'd make sure she knew I heard her. I'd pull up a chair at the beginning of our next class, and I'd listen. That would be the start of K.C.'s doing more than just fine in her freshman English class. I am pretty sure of it.

I'm more than sure I would never have chosen Charles Dickens's novels for a round of book clubs. Poor K.C. and her ninth-grade peers had to deal with my lack of interest in their lives here, too. I completely ignored their largely Hispanic heritage. I may as well have said, "Hey, you get to choose one of these five books, with an average page count of almost six hundred by this White author who lived over a hundred years before you in a place you've probably never been. Not readers, you say? I'll make you read!," as I tapped out five different reading quizzes for the five different books: (1) *Great Expectations* (Dickens, 1861/2002), (2) *David Copperfield* (Dickens, 1850/2004), (3) *Oliver Twist* (Dickens, 1838/2003a), (4) *Nicholas Nickleby* (Dickens, 1839/1999), and (5) *A Tale of Two Cities* (Dickens, 1859/2003b). "And at the end of the unit, we'll all dress up like the characters and drink tea." (Oh yes, we did that.) It was a tale of twisted expectations and not a nickel of authentic reading and writing.

I've heard it a hundred times from well-meaning fellow teachers: "Don't be too hard on yourself. We all learn." Thank God we do. I think about those young people from my first few years of teaching, and I know I wasted valuable time. If do-overs were possible, I would do things differently because I am different now. I know better. I learned to be better.

Source: Adapted from Rasmussen (2018, 2019). Used with permission.

Teaching Readers to Make Choices

As with any academic skill, you must directly teach students how to make choices about their reading before asking them to do so independently. In chapter 2 (page 32), we define book talks as simply putting the spotlight on a given text. Similarly, you might also do story talks, poem talks, and so on. Here's a simple example of a story talk: say you're teaching students about characterization. Instead of having all students read the same story, you might give them a choice of three. You could say, "If you like stories with a female narrator, you might choose this one. If you like stories set in a different era—like the future—you might choose this one. If you've never read a story told from the perspective of a dog, you might choose this one." (Yes, there really are stories told from the perspective of dogs fit for secondary learners.) Now, you've invited students to choose a story they might find more interesting than others—and you've prompted them to think about their preferences of narrator, setting, and perspective (all important literary terms). Both are steps toward young people's owning their learning.

The same approach, or something similar, works for any genre or form of text you want students to read. As another example, say your unit theme is something like this: What does it mean to be courageously human? (This is a common theme in Amy's classroom.) You want your students engaged in reading full-length books that might challenge their abilities a bit, and because they're seniors, you want to ensure they're prepared for the amount of critical reading they will do in college if they go. Rather than assigning a specific text, you meet with the school librarian and ask him or her to pull memoirs, knowing in one way or another, every memoir will relate to the aforementioned theme. You bring all these titles into your classroom and talk to students as they read book covers, look up reviews, and think about which book they are willing to invest their time in. You share some of the thoughts you had as you read some of these books. You talk to students, either individually or as a class, about how readers choose books to read—perhaps thinking aloud and using questions like the following. (Incidentally, these are all questions worth considering as you prepare book talks as well.)

- Does this book interest me because of the narrator? Do I like the voice?
- Am I interested in the setting?
- Do I want to read the story of a person still living or from a different time period? Or of a person from a culture the same as mine or one I'm not familiar with?
- What do I think of the writing style? Do I appreciate the language the author uses, or is it too simplistic, too dull, or too difficult? Do I have to do too much rereading? I may not be able to commit to reading something that slows me down too much.
- Is the book's text in a font size that I will be able to comfortably read?
- After I read the first page, does the book compel me to keep reading? Am I hooked, or at least a little interested?
- Do I like the cover?

In its simplest form, thinking aloud models the skill of self-questioning, which is a necessary skill in making choices and getting students to reflect on and self-assess their learning.

Of course, talking about books in this way with students can be daunting. This is one reason authentic literacy teachers must be readers themselves, as described in chapter 2 (page 21). Literacy teachers know how to talk about books because they read books! They also know titles and texts their students will want to read. Every authentic literacy teacher has a responsibility to grow in this knowledge. You have to know the possibilities so you can help your students choose among them.

Part of this responsibility includes guiding students to make choices that are beneficial for their reading identities. Students need to choose books that are rich in language and global ideas—books that stretch their reading abilities and help them think through moral dilemmas and human conflicts. That's what good books do. And all educators know young people who will walk the easiest road if allowed. So teachers must guide students to make choices that challenge them and benefit their reading identities.

For example, say you have a student who claims to not like reading. This student might choose books you know are easy or lack a sophisticated writing style. You also know this young person loves sports. So you talk about sports books a lot and often. You might introduce several options, reading a short passage from each that shows beautiful imagery or creates tension or excitement. You might talk about what you notice in the authors' styles: "Did you notice the rhythm as I read that? It reads like a ball bouncing on the court. The writer creates that with rapid-fire, short sentences. Or in this one, did you notice the senses the writer weaves into the description of the football field? There's sight and sound and taste and touch all packed into three tight sentences." Again, by modeling and questioning, you can help the student consider choosing a book with a more sophisticated writing style (and depending on the student, you might be the first teacher to teach him or her what style even means).

Sometimes, the first step to ensuring students make their own choices in regard to reading is helping them discover that reading can be a pleasurable activity. Real readers read because they like reading—and they are usually good at it. In many cases, secondary students do not like to read because they do not have the fluency or vocabulary needed to make reading independently interesting. To know a student's fluency and vocabulary, secondary literacy teachers will have to ask the student to read aloud to them—thus, the importance of meeting with readers in one-on-one conferences. We strongly deter you from asking students to read aloud to the class until you are certain they have the fluency and tonality to do so. Such public reading before a student is ready can cause a great detriment to his or her development.

Other times, the first step to ensuring students make their own choices in regard to reading is helping them redefine what it means to be a reader. Sure, some readers read for the aesthetic of it—they like the terror of a Stephen King novel or the tender moments of a Nicholas Sparks. They hoard books, walk around with books, hang out in the school library. They'd rather cozy up with a novel and a cup of tea than go to a social gathering. But there are other kinds of readers. Some readers seek knowledge, wisdom, and understanding—such as how to change a shattered iPhone screen, how to decide a career path, or how to gain followers on social media. Every young person reads when the desire is strong enough. You may have to remind some students, but they will all be able to tell you some topic they learned about through reading, especially if they have a smartphone in their hands. Helping students redefine what they think it means to be a reader can then become an invitation to read more for information or for fun.

All readers, however, no matter their reasons for reading or their choices in reading material, need fundamental skills in regard to comprehension and how language works to create meaning. Your students who come to you as readers, maybe even with library cards and lists of favorite authors, probably don't remember learning these skills. Your students who push back against all things reading? They most likely didn't learn the skills, or at least they didn't learn them well. The most efficient and effective way for secondary literacy teachers to know whether a student has acquired the reading skills needed for sustained self-selected independent reading (see page 114) is to meet with students in one-on-one conferences (see chapter 6, page 99, for more on conferring).

If teachers show their knowledge about books and enthusiastically share how writers create scenes, characters, meaningful dialogue, and everything else great writers do, students who claim to hate reading, like the sports lover, will learn how to choose books they *want* to read—and those books may powerfully impact their identities as readers. See "Talking to Readers About Books" to plan and practice teaching readers to make choices.

Reader Reflection: *Talking to Readers About Books*

Think about a book you want to share with your readers. This can be *the* book that made you a reader (most people who like to read can name a specific title that began instilling this identity), or it can be a book you recently read or one you liked when you were in school. Then, use the following tips to plan how you would present this book as a choice for your students to read.

- Plan in advance.
- Speak with certainty and enthusiasm.
- Highlight the author and any awards the author has won: ______________________
- Make it interesting; consider sharing the following about the book.
    - Why you liked it: ______________________
    - What you learned from it: ______________________
    - How it made you feel: ______________________
    - Why it made you think: ______________________
- Engage readers with ELA content vocabulary.
    - Read aloud the first paragraph; note the narrator's voice: ______________________
    - Read aloud a significant or poignant passage; explain why it's significant or poignant as related to theme: ______________________
    - Describe the characters: ______________________
    - Explain the conflict: ______________________
    - Point out any unique structure: ______________________
- Keep it short (two to four minutes is optimal).

Note: Keeping book talks short can be a challenge (thus the importance of planning in advance). While all the suggestions in this list will certainly help you introduce books students may choose to read, remember not to talk too much. You'll need to make choices about when and how you share books with your readers.

Visit ***go.SolutionTree.com/literacy*** *for a free reproducible version of this reflection.*

Teaching Writers to Make Choices

Now, we need to talk about writing. In authentic literacy classrooms, students also make choices about writing. Students don't need the narrow essay prompts or prompts designed to imitate standardized tests, both of which are so common in secondary ELA classrooms. A prompt such as "Write about a time you were loyal" is hardly conducive to teenagers' writing with commitment and a desire to improve as writers. They need literacy teachers to catalyze their thinking so they remember experiences and memories and so they can create their own prompts.

Just as self-selected independent reading (see page 114) is an integral part of authentic literacy instruction, so is low-stakes, stress-free writing—what we call *response writing*. Literacy students should be writing responses daily. Depending on the length of the class period, students might write for five to fifteen minutes. We suggest keeping the time short until students develop some writing endurance. This writing practice is different from freewriting, where students simply write for a given amount of time. Response writing is targeted toward learning goals and is potentially more purposeful for individual writers. It serves a variety of valuable purposes, such as writing to think, clarify, remember, make connections, support ideas, or challenge them. In response writing, the student writer him- or herself is the audience. Writers write first for themselves. They write to understand themselves before they write to be understood. Once student writers are well aware of writing's influence on the self, they can find a greater purpose of writing to influence others instead of simply writing to complete a task.

Broadly speaking, the approach that we recommend involves three elements. First, writers need a notebook or other place to collect ideas that they may want to explore and develop later. Second, writers need frequent opportunities to practice low-stakes, stress-free writing in their notebooks—that is, to collect ideas without worry about grades. Students should be writing in abundance, and the teacher will never read most of their writing. When students respond personally and reflectively, they often write as exploration of ideas—snippets of thought they could eventually utilize for a future composition. Thus, you guide students in the daily routine of stress-free written response as a means for them to collect ideas worth expanding on and sharing with an audience. Finally, when an assignment or more formal writing is called for, writers choose topics from their cache of ideas, rather than from a narrow, teacher-provided prompt. Their chosen ideas lead to their making other choices about their writing as they learn and practice within their writers' notebooks specific literary devices, rhetorical strategies, and skills—the options for written expression that real writers apply depending on their intended meaning and the audience they want to influence. For example, a response-writing piece about how a student personally feels about an image from the news could blossom into a full-blown persuasive essay. On the other hand, when a student responds to an article based on textual evidence, that type of response may spark the student to further inquire into the topic, leading to research-based argument writing.

In the following sections, we share two approaches to response writing and discuss teaching lessons on the craft of writing, which students will apply as they write in more formal contexts.

Personal Response Writing

In this section, we share an overview of how we facilitate *personal response writing*. (This builds on the discussion of Inviting Personal Reactions, page 48.) Sparking ideas for students to write about can be as simple or complex as you want it to be. Maybe you want students to think about a theme you'll explore in a story you'll read later in class, so you read a few stanzas from a poem with a similar theme. Maybe you want them to practice analyzing information, so you project an infographic. Maybe you want them to gather stories from their lives, so you pose a couple of questions related to their childhoods. The basic premise is to stimulate student thought.

To ask students to write their thinking, you must first establish expectations. Before introducing this strategy for the first time, explain the following to students.

- Writers make choices about audience, topic, form, structure, word choice, device, and so on.
- Writers write more than they will ever publish. Volume writing helps build stamina and fluency, can help with making decisions regarding topic and craft, and may help build prior knowledge about topics and themes explored in class.
- Writers often produce their best writing when they write from their lives and about what is personal. Thinking about a topic can help writers remember experiences and events in their lives, explore ideas related to the topic, and discover new ideas.
- In personal response writing, it's OK to not be perfect. There is no perfection in writing, anyway. Writers play with language as they formulate their ideas on the page. They also read over what they write and try to make it better.

Each time you employ personal response writing in your classroom, use the following steps.

1. Select a stimulus text. You might choose spoken-word or other forms of poetry, song lyrics, short news articles, infographics, tweets, videos, posts by influencers, or, of course, excerpts from books in your classroom library. The goal is to create exigency in student writers, a reason to respond—like an itch they need to scratch as they generate ideas on the page.
2. Instruct students to read or watch the stimulus text. Set a timer and have them write for five to ten minutes. They should write as much as they can as fast as they can as well as they can. Ask them to think about experiences, situations, events, or conflicts that might relate to whatever theme of the text you use to spark this initial thinking.
3. At the end of the time, ask students to read over their writing and make changes that clarify and improve it. Be sure you model how to do this. Consider projecting your writing, so students can see what you've written and how you make changes.
4. Finally, ask student writers to read what they wrote to one another. This reinforces the imperative of building a community of trust—this is a vulnerable act. Remind students to actually read aloud exactly what they wrote

on the page, rather than telling their partners what they wrote about. Reading one's writing out loud often helps the writer see areas for improvement immediately.

Have students write personal responses as often as your schedule allows. The more ideas students have stockpiled in their notebooks, the more choice they have when it comes to making decisions about topics they want to write about for their compositions.

Text-Based Response Writing

Prior to, during, or after reading or watching a text with your class, you may provide some kind of stimulus and ask students to respond to the text, with the specific instructions to use evidence from the text, either quoted or paraphrased, to support their thinking. This text-based response requires greater skill than personal response writing—students will need to know how to embed quotes or paraphrase—skills you may teach prior to this response writing in targeted short bursts of direct teaching. To practice text-based response, you will need to model the thinking you do as you read the text, along with how you structure your thoughts on the page as you write. For most text-based response writing, students will still write in their notebooks. Remember, the notebook is a safe place for students to play with their ideas, practice craft moves as they learn from other writers, and practice specific skills you teach them as they relate to your objectives. All are part of a collection that helps them become better writers.

What can text-based response writing look like? Here's an example. Say the learning objective relates to helping students analyze bias in a text. First, you may want to know if students read critically enough to even identify bias. You would purposefully select one or more texts that show various levels of bias the writers sprinkle throughout the piece. Prior to reading the whole of the text, you might select just one sentence or one paragraph to use as a stimulus for response. After reading this short excerpt, you'd ask students to write a response wherein they use evidence from the text to support their thinking. Then, simply ask questions: "What does this statement make you think or feel? Do you think the writer shows bias, and why or why not?" Of course, as with any writing you ask students to do, you write, too, modeling your thinking either before or after they write their responses and sometimes using your own response as a model text (see page 83).

Each time you employ text-based response writing in your classroom, you will encourage the same four actions as detailed in personal response writing (read, write, edit, and share; page 63) with one added instruction: be sure to use text evidence, either directly quoting or paraphrasing the text, to support your thinking.

Utilizing personal response writing and text-based response writing in equal measure is important for your writers. You may feel compelled to spend more class time on text-based writing for a number of reasons—preparation for high-stakes exams, for example. Please use caution. When students engage regularly in personal response writing and share their writing with their peers, the reciprocal values of trust and vulnerability strengthen relationships, support your learning community, and lead to greater student ownership of their learning. Text-based writing can do this to some degree, but the topics are often much less personal in nature. If the balance of writing veers too far away from topics and ideas that relate to students' lived experiences, cultures, and backgrounds, you may lose the time spent purposefully building relationships and growing a community where students stay personally interested and self-motivated to participate. When planning how your students will spend the limited time you have with them, continually ask yourself: "Which practice is more in line with what authentic readers and writers do to improve their skills as accomplished readers and writers?" Then, do those things.

Remember, authentic literacy teachers model the writing experiences they want their student writers to undertake. When students write low-stakes responses, teachers write too—perhaps you even project a passage of your writing on the board. Then, share your thought process as you wrote—what things worked and why some things didn't. Make your thinking visible. Then, when your class has done several rounds of initial thinking in this type of low-stress writing, model how to choose topics to explore further, or select texts you've started and want to craft, publish, and share. See "Engaging in Personal Response Writing" to try out this strategy yourself.

Reader Reflection: *Engaging in Personal Response Writing*

Read the following excerpt from *The Red Bandanna* by Tom Rinaldi (2016), and then write a response in your writing notebook. Consider answering the questions the narrator poses, or just write what the ideas here make you think.

> Take a moment.
>
> Take it out. Unfold it. Press your hand down upon it and flatten it, into the surface of your desk, or the edge of the bed, or along the line of your leg. Twenty-two inches along any side, four ounces in your hand, barely enough weight to notice. Polyester and cotton, dyed and printed, cut and packaged, folded and shipped, to reach you, one way or another, and land in your palm.
>
> Pick it up. Look at it.
>
> What do you see there, in the red, white, and black? Is there something in the ancient pattern and the Persian fig shape, the paisley teardrop and the flat pointed stars? A child's thing, a trifle, a rag?
>
> What do you carry, what truth could it possibly contain? What meaning could it hold?
>
> Fear and strength. Smoke and blood. Doubt and faith. Terror and valor. The dead and the maimed. The way out and the walk down. The sacrifice given, and the salvation granted. Living. Dying.
>
> "It's all in there," the father says. "It's all in that bandanna." (p. 5)

Visit ***go.SolutionTree.com/literacy*** *for a free reproducible version of this reflection.*

Lessons on Craft

When students become aware of writing as an influential tool, they begin thinking about their audience, purpose, and language—and this drives their decision making about who they will write for, what they will write about, and how they will write. Knowing that writing is influential empowers student writers to make choices. Pleasure and passion come from knowing one's writing has influence, and student writers need to have this experience. They should leave high school confident that the choices they make as writers can be powerful tools as they navigate their lives, whether they're writing cover letters for job applications, business proposals to financiers, emails to potential clients, reflections in a daily journal, or posts on social media. Writing *is* influential. Student writers in authentic literacy classrooms have the potential to shape the world with their pens and keyboards. They will if teachers guide them in their freedom to make effective choices as they write. To make effective choices, students (with their teachers working as fellow writers) must study texts in order to understand the craft of writing. This intense study of how writers craft meaning can help them become more skilled writers and even help their comprehension as they read independently (Kittle, 2013).

As you transform your teaching, be on the lookout for rich texts with identifiable author's craft moves. You can use these as stimulus for personal and text-based response writing, as well as for teaching students about the choices that authors make in their writing. As students grow in their analysis of author's craft, they can help you find other texts worthy of craft study. When students identify craft moves, that's one thing. When they come to you eager to share a passage that speaks to them as a writer, that's a whole new world of excitement as an authentic literacy teacher.

A robust classroom library is the perfect resource for finding texts worthy of intense study; however, other rich texts are readily available online, and many teachers share them frequently on Twitter and other social media sites—employ your personal learning network. Like you learned in chapter 2 (page 21), when you broaden your scope and develop your own identity as a reader and writer, you will see texts through the lens of the authentic literacy expert you're becoming, and you will know how to use them. Using excerpts from books in your classroom library and other rich texts as instructional tools serves the following purposes that help learners identify more fully as authentic readers and writers.

- Giving you an opportunity to highlight a specific book or author (like a bonus book talk)
- Helping your students see that authors make choices about how they craft meaning
- Providing in-context examples of grammatical structures or literary devices needed for your skills-based instruction
- Inviting students to talk to one another about the books they are reading as they learn to recognize author's craft in their own self-selected books
- Allowing students to learn from one another as they discuss, analyze, and evaluate how writers craft meaning in a variety of texts

So what might a text study look like in practical application? Here's one example: Let's say you are teaching students to write personal narratives, but they are struggling to open their pieces with anything other than a knock at the door or the buzzing of the alarm clock. (Like us, you've likely read your fair share of essays that start this way.) You can use books self-selected by students for their independent reading to show your students options for their own writing—specifically, different ways published authors begin narratives. What follows are three examples, pulled from YA fiction books in Amy's classroom library. Read them and think about how you could use these excerpts, or ones similar, to help your students make choices about how to begin their narratives. Consider the following guiding questions as you think through these text selections.

- What information does the author share? How does he or she share this information (interesting word choice, unique sentence structure, descriptive language, and so on)?
- What mood does the author create?
- What about the opening compels the reader to keep reading?

First, examine the opening of *Turtles All the Way Down* by John Green (2019).

> At the time I first realized I might be fictional, my weekdays were spent at a publicly funded institution on the north side of Indianapolis called White River High School, where I was required to eat lunch at a particular time—between 12:37 p.m. and 1:14 p.m.—by forces so much larger than myself that I couldn't even begin to identify them. If those forces had given me a different lunch period, or if the tablemates who helped author my fate had chosen a different topic of conversation that September day, I would've met a different end—or at least a different middle. But I was beginning to learn that your life is a story told about you, not one that you tell. (p. 1)

Next, *In Darkness* by Nick Lake (2012) begins as follows.

> I am the voice in the dark, calling out for your help.
>
> I am the quiet voice that you hope will not turn to silence, the voice you want to keep hearing cos it means someone is still alive. I am the voice calling for you to come and dig me out. I am the voice in the dark, asking you to unbury me, to bring me from the grave out into the light, like a zombie.
>
> I am a killer and I have been killed, too, over and over; I am constantly being born. I have lost more things than I have found; I have destroyed more things than I have built. I have seen babies abandoned in the trash and I have seen the dead come back to life.
>
> I first shot a man when I was twelve years old. (p. 1)

Finally, here are the opening paragraphs from *The Thing About Jellyfish* by Ali Benjamin (2015):

> A jellyfish, if you watch it long enough, begins to look like a heart beating. It doesn't matter what kind: the blood-red *Atolla* with its flashing siren lights, the frilly flower hat variety, or the near-transparent moon jelly, *Aurelia aurita*. It's their pulse, the way they contract swiftly, then release. Like a ghost heart—a heart you can see right through, right into some other world where everything you ever lost has gone to hide.
>
> Jellyfish don't even have hearts, of course—no heart, no brain, no bone, no blood. But watch them for a while. You will see them beating.

> Mrs. Turton says that if you lived to be eighty years old, your heart would beat three billion times. I was thinking about that, trying to imagine a number that large. Three *billion*. Count back three billion hours, and modern humans don't exist—just wild-eyed cave people, all hairy and grunting. Three billion years, and life itself barely exists. And yet here's your heart, doing its job all the time, one beat after the next, all the way up to three billion.
>
> But only if you get to live that long. (p. 1)

How did you answer the guiding questions? Perhaps you noticed that the information each author reveals is similar—readers learn the identity of the narrator (who is also the protagonist in these examples), something interesting about this character, and some kind of conflict the narrator is facing. Plus, the authors establish some kind of interesting mood, projected through the narrator's voice. Authors routinely reveal these elements (and sometimes setting) in the first few paragraphs of most pieces of YA fiction, which of course is narrative—and this takes us back to the personal narrative essay your theoretical students are writing. You would use these texts, or mentor texts like them, to teach students how other writers make their introductions interesting. Prompt them to read and study introductions, see what they notice about the information the authors reveal, how they reveal that information, and so on. Given time and modeling by you, students can then turn to their self-selected books and read to notice how those writers made choices as they composed compelling introductions that made their readers want to keep reading.

Using short excerpts like these sample texts as instructional materials and then asking students to turn to their own books for other examples solidifies the integration of reading and writing instruction. It helps readers not only comprehend what they read (What did you learn about the character, the conflict, and the setting?) but also understand how writers craft meaning (How did the author introduce the character, the conflict, and the setting?). Now, student writers have options—perhaps a whole classroom library full of them—for how they might choose to begin their own personal narratives. The same process of using excerpts works for teaching most any literary device, rhetorical strategy, or writerly choice.

The hope of authentic literacy teachers is that all students become independent, self-identified readers and writers. So students must practice independence every day while they have the opportunity. An independent reader, writer, thinker, and communicator knows how to transfer the skills he or she learns from text to text and task to task. For example, the students who once struggled to start their narratives now know they can read and study how other writers start narratives. They can transfer this skill of critical reading to any other mode of writing they may undertake in their educational careers and beyond: What do other writers do to start a personal statement, or a biographical sketch, or a business letter? They know to seek out examples and make choices like other confident writers do.

Throughout the writing process, remember this: writers make choices. Not only do they choose topics, they choose audiences, structures, and all the elements that craft tone. Real writers make decisions, but in our experience, few secondary student writers know they can—and should—make decisions as they write. Authentic writing teachers intend not to make the choices for students but to guide, teach, and model the choices writers make as developing student writers learn to make their own. It's a high bar, but when teachers build and sustain personal relationships in communities of trust, students will rise to high expectations. Will you sometimes have to nudge them into tackling challenges or doing more? Of course. But as you guide and encourage, provoke, and continually model, your learners will begin to take on the responsibility for their own literacy learning. And when they bring you their self-selected book with pages open wide so you can see the craft they've noticed in an author's writing, and they excitedly describe it to you and maybe even tell their friends, that's gold right there.

Summary

As authentic literacy teachers, devoted to teaching the skills all students need to excel in their literacy lives, let's stop spending time teaching isolated texts instead of readers; let's stop assigning rote tasks instead of authentic tasks that real readers and writers undertake. Students deserve to make choices about their learning. They need the engagement and the buy-in. They need to know their teachers care about them as individuals with unique interests, ideas, and passions. Opening space for students to make choices accomplishes all of this—and more.

When teachers offer choices in reading and writing instruction based on what intrinsically motivates students to learn (namely, books and topics they personally select), and then teach and model the thinking required to analyze what and how others write, instruction becomes at once more learner friendly and increasingly sophisticated and challenging. This is instruction that converts student interest and motivation into application of skills and ownership for transfer. Adolescent readers who at one time claimed to hate reading may find books that help them solve personal problems or influence them to research and find solutions to social or world issues. Filling their notebooks with topics and ideas they care about can help young adults see writing as an exercise in clearing their heads and discovering ideas they'd never before imagined. Literacy is power. Imagine the possibilities for wonder and achievement when students feel an energy to learn like they may have never felt before. Making choices about their reading and writing can spark this energy, and setting this renewable energy as a goal is a significant reason to offer students choice in secondary literacy classrooms and teach them to make effective choices along their educational journey.

Your Turn: Chapter 4

Reflecting on what you've learned in this chapter, record your primary action steps. As an authentic literacy teacher, I will:

-
-

Teaching adolescents to become readers and writers can be a challenging goal. Anyone who's spent much time with adolescents in schools knows this well. Consider the quote accredited to Joseph Campbell, "The job of an educator is to teach students to see vitality in themselves" (Goodreads, n.d.), and think about the content of this chapter in relation to your practice. Then, choose one of the following questions, and write a response as if your students are your audience. Share your writing with a colleague or your students—or with your book study group.

- How might opening up space for students to make choices about their learning help you "teach students to see vitality in themselves" and write about that vitality?
- Think about the choices you were allowed to make in your secondary English language arts and reading classes. How did these choices help, or not help, you want to learn?
- Students have varying interests, talents, and needs when it comes to literacy. How can offering students their choice of books from a robust classroom library help you instruct individuals in more effective and efficient ways than continually selecting whole-class texts?

CHAPTER 5

Student Application of Literacy Skills

So far, we have looked at conditions that encourage authentic literacy practices to take root, including the importance of teacher expertise, relationships and community, and student choice. In this chapter, we focus on what authentic literacy teachers are ultimately striving to accomplish. They constantly drive for learners to become more independent thinkers, readers, writers, and communicators. The goal of authentic literacy practices is for students to walk away able to apply and transfer critical skills for thinking, reading, writing, and communicating. It's not enough for secondary students to simply know some things about literacy; instead, they should graduate aware of and able to apply their literacy skills to any situation they encounter in college, in their careers, and as valuable participants in their communities.

Thus, authentic literacy teachers must ensure that students can transfer what they have learned to multiple contexts via their thinking, reading, writing, and communicating. Students must develop ownership of their learning so that they can apply it dynamically to influence the world around them. Gholdy Muhammad (2020) puts it this way in her book *Cultivating Genius: An Equity Framework for Culturally and Historically Responsive Literacy*: "Literacy is not just about reading words on the page; it also carries some sort of action. In other words, reading and writing are transformative acts that improve self and society" (pp. 9–10).

Classroom relationships and student choice (chapters 3 and 4, pages 37 and 51) help students develop intrinsic motivation for literacy. Teachers must first recognize and then leverage intrinsic motivation to guide students to become increasingly self-aware of their thinking, actions, and communication. As self-awareness or metacognition increases, so does learners' ability to intentionally take ownership of their thinking—which is often made visible through writing and communication. When learners increasingly own their learning, they begin to authentically apply it to new concepts and contexts—essentially, transferring learning from text to text and task to task while increasingly engaging in authentic inquiry. Figure 5.1 (page 72) illustrates how all of these complex aspects of learning are inexorably linked in an authentic literacy classroom.

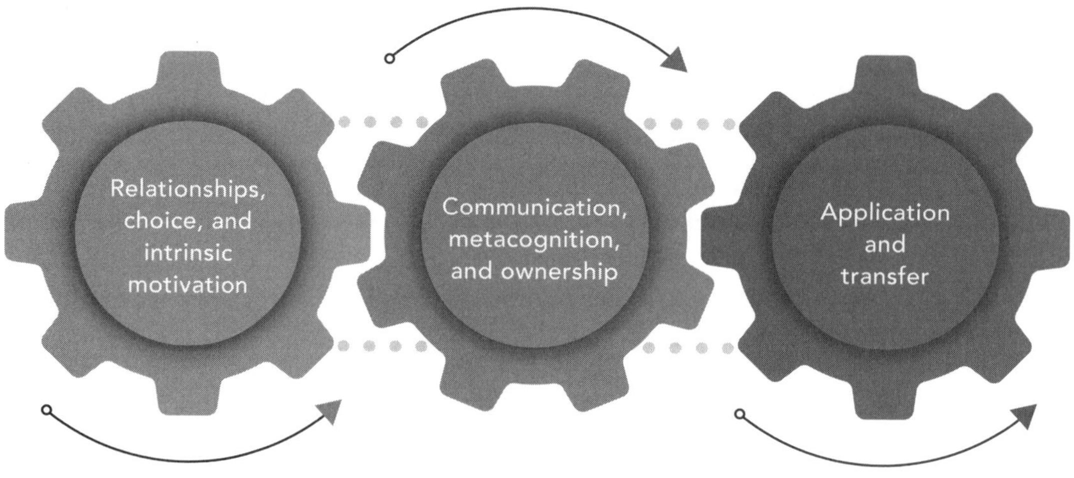

Figure 5.1: Precursors that drive application and transfer.

Achieving student transfer and independent application of skills, what Fisher and colleagues (2016) call "the ultimate goal" (p. 21), is not a linear sequence. It's a complicated reciprocal process that is ongoing for all learners—including teachers. As figure 5.1 illustrates, aspects like intrinsic motivation, communication, metacognition, and ownership lead to students' ability to independently, authentically, and successfully transfer and apply skills to new scenarios and situations. As they transfer and apply skills to new scenarios and situations, space opens up to engage them in authentic inquiry practices. Relationships and choice are the engine that makes this work run. However, the process of driving learners' thinking toward independent application and transfer of skills isn't automatic. There isn't one formula for success, and it isn't a singular event. It's a recursive, ongoing process that authentic literacy educators weave in and out of, in conjunction with unique learners, throughout each year, often with very different learners. Nevertheless, it is the goal to continuously strive for. In this chapter, we detail aspects of authentic literacy that move toward application, as well as strategies to help students along their journey (accompanied by honesty about some of the challenges along the way).

Amy's Reflections From the Field

"Mrs. Ras, you've made me a nerd," Alejandra said as she came into the room. "I read this whole book over the weekend, and my sister told me I was weird."

Sometimes, the best surprises come from stories like Alejandra's. She was a hard case at the beginning of the semester. Like her friends, all comfortable at the table farthest from the front, Alejandra was a self-proclaimed nonreader. Even though we'd built a pretty solid community where everyone got along and at least outwardly practiced our literacy routines, we had not become a community of readers. Alejandra's little group was a holdout, and it had a lot of social clout that influenced almost every other student in the large class. I had spent a lot of time talking about books I thought they'd find interesting and talking to them one-on-one with the hope of having some kind of book breakthrough—so much so that I finally realized I was spending too much time with these students and not enough time with others. I decided to ignore them. As long as they were quiet while everyone else read during self-selected independent reading time, I let them be.

Alejandra couldn't stand it. She started asking me questions about books in our classroom library. Then, she started asking other friends about books. She started going to the school library, and once she found one book she really liked, she wanted more. In class, Alejandra wanted to read—and she wanted her friends to let her read, and some of them even let her.

Sarah was a different matter. She already liked to read. "I like historical fiction, I guess, but you know, *real,*" she told me with a shrug during our first chat, "and I really just want to be done with this class and out of this school." She pushed back against everything I did, and everything I said. She really just wanted to be left alone. Until, all of a sudden, she didn't. Sarah went from the sullen young woman who never spoke to her tablemates and never engaged in class discussions and never even looked at me if she could help it to a vivacious and voracious writer. I had no idea why.

When the time was right, I asked Sarah about her change in attitude. She told me mine was the first class she'd ever had where she felt like she was in control. "You talk to us like adults—like you really want us to be successful in life," she said. "You push without being pushy, and you let us choose books we like. And you make us write a lot, but you never tell us what to write. I never thought I wanted to go to college—you know, I told you I was just gonna get a job—but now, I think I do. And I think I'm going to study marine biology, which is something I always wanted but didn't think would ever be possible." She'd jumped from slogging through the steps needed to graduate high school to wanting to explore a career in marine biology? I was stunned! I'd kept to the routines that govern the learning in my classroom. We'd read a lot—books students chose for themselves. We'd written a lot—about topics students wanted to express and explore. We'd talked a lot—about issues circling the adult world my students would soon step into and the skills they'd need to be ready. I didn't know what, but something had clicked for Sarah, and she wanted more.

Both Alejandra and Sarah validated what I've come to know about intrinsic motivation in the classroom. Students find it in different ways—Alejandra because she needed me to see and talk with her, and Sarah because she needed to be left alone to experience learning on her terms and in her own way. There's no magic to this authentic literacy work. There's just consistency in the hard work that helps students want to learn in real ways about real things that matter to them personally.

Intrinsic Motivation

Although we wrote about the need for intrinsic motivation to drive learning forward in the previous chapter (page 51), the reality is not every secondary literacy student willingly embraces the authentic literacy habits we want for them. In fact, many of them resist making choices, avoid engaging in learning community relationships, and shy away from transparently writing and communicating about their thinking. Yet authentic literacy educators continue to routinely engage and challenge learners to grow, striving to discover what intrinsically motivates them. Fortunately, most adolescent learners respond to challenge if teachers are thoughtful about the conditions they create. As John Hattie and Shirley Clarke (2019) point out:

> Students will often willingly undertake very challenging tasks if they find them engaging, want to strive to succeed, have a good sense of what it means to be successful and know a set of strategies for when they get stuck. (p. 15)

It is the teacher's job to engage students and motivate them to strive for success—being explicit about what success can look like through modeling while providing them tools to use independently. Conditions should be challenging but not frustrating, induce growth but not allow too much comfort or ease. Essentially, these conditions are the pathways to opportunities for deep learning—application and transfer. Teachers can set students along these paths by challenging their thinking.

Challenge makes learning fun. Most learners enjoy thinking critically, engaging in discussion, and, yes, even working hard when they feel the tug of intrinsic motivation to the task at hand. Teachers need to identify and cultivate this tug, and when it comes to reading and writing, they sometimes have to create the tug. In chapter 4 (page 51), we wrote extensively about the importance of ensuring that you empower learners to make choices related to their interests, what they find relevant, and their identities. Engaging students through personalized choices is a significant way to create the tug of motivation, often because they find the work personally beneficial.

To help students invest the thought and time necessary to learn at high levels, teachers must not just build relationships with students (as discussed in chapter 3, page 37). They must also challenge students to take ownership of their learning and to begin independently making connections across their learning contexts—a necessary step toward the independent application and transfer of skills. As Michael McDowell (2020) points out in his book *Teaching for Transfer*, "What students are searching for in this process is the actual relationship between different contexts" (p. 46). This is another way to create the tug for learners: help them become aware of how critical literacy skills apply to and enhance their engagement with other contexts they are interested in. For example, you might guide learners to write about community involvement and advocacy if they are interested in being involved in broader social issues.

To build on this, frame learning in inquiry (a process of questioning, exploring, evaluating, and extending) and discovery, and model how real readers and writers think about their processes and how they pose questions that lead to exploration and growth. In essence, in authentic literacy classrooms, thinking and inquiry become ongoing reciprocal processes; the more one asks questions and seeks answers, the more one learns there is more to learn. And the more one independently applies new learning to relevant and meaningful topics and tasks, the more deeply one consolidates the learning and transfers it to where it will make an impact.

Intrinsically motivated students move into what Fisher and colleagues (2016) call "deep consolidation" (p. 92). These learners embrace the personal, vulnerable, risky nature of applying new skills, and transfer their learning to new and relevant tasks—such as writing about a challenging but personally important issue, reading a book deemed "too difficult," or writing an essay in a unique structure or form. In short, when students are intrinsically motivated, they begin to think about their thinking, and they begin to propel their own learning experiences. They begin to become self-aware, self-driven, and self-directed learners who ask questions and seek out the answers.

Intrinsic motivation can be difficult to tap into, but it's a necessary element of the transfer of learning—which is the ultimate goal and indicates you can feel confident that learning is taking root (Fisher et al., 2016). At the heart of educators' craft should be the question, What intrinsically motivates students to deeply consolidate their learning and maintain the ability to transfer it to new texts and tasks? And more specific to authentic literacy practitioners, What intrinsically motivates readers, writers, and communicators to delve deeply into their craft and apply their literacy skills? See "Reflecting on Motivation" to help you better understand your current approach to student motivation.

Reader Reflection: *Reflecting on Motivation*

The idea that motivation is a key component to student learning isn't new. But how teachers go about motivating students can vary from practices that are very extrinsic to ones that are more intrinsic.

Use the following T-chart template to list the tools and practices you've used in the past to extrinsically and intrinsically motivate students, and compare the two sides of your chart. Then, think about which practices do a better job of fostering student ownership of learning and independent application.

Intrinsically Motivating Tools and Practices	Extrinsically Motivating Tools and Practices

Students' interests are a powerful motivator. Think about the students you are teaching or have taught in the recent past. What do you know about them? What do they care about? Make a list of some topics that students care about and how these could spark intrinsic motivation in your authentic literacy classroom. Think of topics that are personal, relevant, interesting, meaningful, curious, impactful, and attainable.

continued ▶

Students' Interests	How the Interests Could Intrinsically Motivate Students

Visit ***go.SolutionTree.com/literacy*** *for a free reproducible version of this reflection.*

Metacognition

As students gain motivation and start down the path toward application, teachers can introduce metacognition, or self-awareness of thinking and choices. Fisher and colleagues (2016) explain, "Deep learners are able to think metacognitively, take action, discuss ideas, and see errors as a necessary part of learning" (p. 75). Developing this skill early in their progression toward independent application and transfer prepares students to learn from struggle. When students are applying and transferring skills independently, errors will occur. Teachers can plan to be responsive to such errors and help students see them as a chance to grow. Authentic literacy teachers provide opportunities for students to learn from trying and testing ideas—and from failing—as they apply increasingly sophisticated skills. This rigorous learning requires sustained metacognition, driven by intrinsic motivation and made visible through writing and communication that inspire learning and connections beyond the classroom walls.

First, teachers help students think about their thinking. You might even teach students the term *metacognition*. When you help students recognize and analyze the thinking they do as they learn, you help them understand that deeper thinking leads to deeper learning. As Fisher and colleagues (2016) describe, "Students [learn] how to plan, organize, elaborate, and reflect" as "they further consolidate through self-talk and self-questioning, both of which are necessary to becoming increasingly aware of their own metacognition" (p. 76).

Often, this metacognition begins with the thinking processes that learners need to become more deeply aware of, because their thoughts impact their reading, writing, and communicating choices. During direct instruction or a minilesson, for example, teachers challenge learners' thinking to grow by modeling expert thinking aloud through complex reading and writing processes. A teacher might think aloud about why a writer chose a particular rhetorical device to intentionally influence the essay's audience to consider a new idea or position. A teacher might also think aloud about how the beauty of a poem's language makes her feel and how it might make her react, respond, or reflect as a result. The purpose of teachers' sharing their self-awareness and metacognition through modeling and thinking aloud is to ultimately provoke that same thinking in learners.

Student Ownership

In our experience, student ownership of literacy learning is made visible through the writing process; after all, writing is an act of creation—if literacy educators allow it to be. Too often, literacy educators constrain writing—a unique creative act—by requiring strict formulas and criteria. And, while having criteria for quality writing is important so students know what their learning targets are, guiding or limiting the writing process too much can be detrimental. Instead, teachers should promote writing autonomy, within focused criteria for quality writing—modeling writing and guiding students along the way as the expert writers in the classroom.

Teachers can have confidence in student ownership when they observe students transfer skills to multiple thinking and writing tasks. Ownership is especially demonstrated in writing because students display deep consolidation of learning through a task that is rooted in self-dependency instead of teacher dependency. Student ownership is apparent when it is the students making the writing choices—choices that challenge them, demonstrate that they know their strengths and limits, reveal their passions and areas for growth, and indicate the areas in the world that they know they can impact for the better.

Writers who demonstrate ownership of their learning do the following.

- Make choices about the issues and ideas they write about
- Choose to write about issues and ideas that are deeply personal
- Understand that writing impacts oneself and an audience
- Notice the moves other writers use, and employ or imitate the moves in their own writing
- Publish and share their writing to influence individuals and society

We wrote extensively in chapter 4 (page 51) about the need for student choice, based on the premise that reading is pleasurable and writing is influential. We then went on to recognize the important link between choice and intrinsic motivation, all of which leads to application via the transfer of skills to new tasks. The seminal transfer that occurs in an authentic literacy classroom is the network among listening, speaking, reading, writing, and thinking. For example, thinking happens based on reading, writing is created related to what's read, and communication about ideas heard, thought, read, and written happens all along the way.

Traditionally, the most challenging transfer to accomplish is to link writing with listening, speaking, reading, and thinking. Writing continues to be an educational enigma—an incredibly complex skill to teach. As literacy professor and researcher Steven Graham (2018) points out, "Individual writers are not exact replicas of each other" (p. 234). Yet effective writers have similar traits. And we've seen students grow as writers, in an authentic literacy classroom, when they have opportunities to link their own writing to what they notice other writers doing to affect readers—and they then use some of those same writing techniques.

Authentic Inquiry

When a teacher increases students' awareness of their thinking and motivates them to follow their questions through a process of inquiry and discovery, he or she elevates students' ability to independently apply their thinking and skills to new ideas and issues they find relevant and interesting. Authentic inquiry is centered on students—their ideas, questions, worries, problems, and interests. Authentic inquiry isn't about making students step toward what teachers want; it's about listening to them and taking steps in their direction. It's about noticing and using what they know about themselves as readers and writers. It's about helping them question and employ what they see other writers do while using texts as mentors and then exploring new ideas in different texts.

Fundamentally, the goal of authentic inquiry is to teach students to question the world around them. In fact, McDowell (2020) writes, "How we see the world, other people, and ourselves differently and respond based on new ideas, or old ideas viewed differently, is a major part of transfer learning" (p. 57). What McDowell is pointing out is one of the most significant learning outcomes literacy teachers can accomplish. The problem is, far too often in school, teachers dictate to students what they should or shouldn't question or follow a path of inquiry about.

In order to promote the kind of inquiry and research-based writing that students will need to master for college and a multitude of careers, teachers must guide students to find inquiry personal, relevant, meaningful, impactful, and connected to the intrinsic motivations teachers have worked so hard to foster. Next, authentic inquiry involves exploring and evaluating students' ideas, including the opinions and facts shared by other writers and communicators. When students learn to evaluate others' ideas and opinions, they learn to think beyond the surface-level messages being conveyed. Students need to evaluate writers' purpose and intended audience. They should evaluate writers' use of language and rhetoric to influence readers. And, especially, they must evaluate the credibility, biases, and even logical fallacies writers use to affect their readers. All of this contributes to learners' ability to engage in critical inquiry, which informs the ways they communicate and write about the things that interest and motivate them to explore and influence the world around them.

Giving students time to explore their reading and writing identities provides literacy teachers with opportunities to identify the ideas and issues that students feel are worth exploring through reading, further inquiry, and ultimately writing. The process for writing, inquiry, and research isn't a perfect linear equation. The very essence of authentic reading and writing means that students (and even teachers) won't have every question answered at the outset. It's a recursive, personal process that involves plenty of errors, mistakes, and struggles to figure out exactly what the writer is trying to say to him- or herself and to audiences. This means that you have to encourage each individual student to *try* to discover what is relevant, worthwhile, and credible. And *trying* is going to be messy.

Struggle and Errors

At this point, we must acknowledge that everything we've written about in this chapter is complex, complicated work, often fraught with struggles. If students are to authentically own their learning, then that ownership includes the errors and mistakes they must learn from. Teachers can invite students to see risks, struggles, and mistakes as opportunities to learn by modeling taking risks, struggling, and making mistakes as learners themselves. Demonstrating vulnerability and the work it takes to learn from experiences (positive or negative) is key to authentic literacy, inquiry, and ultimate ownership.

No one enjoys making mistakes or struggling, right? Yet some would go so far as to describe struggling as a privilege because it fosters growth and change and leads to innovation and evolution (Cambourne, 1988). And Fisher and colleagues (2016) write:

> Students appreciate challenge. They expect to work hard to achieve success in school and life. When tasks become too easy, students get bored. Similarly, when tasks become too difficult, students get frustrated. There is a sweet spot for learning, but the problem is that it differs for different students. (p. 21)

So, here is the paradox: productive struggle is good; struggle to frustration is bad. The line between good and bad struggle changes from student to student. Does this mean that you can never know where to meet students to help them each struggle productively? No. It only reinforces the importance of and need for authentic relationships, choice, and ownership. The bottom line, though, is that students struggle to engage in a process of applying and transferring skills to new tasks and contexts if they haven't first found the value of taking risks and learning from errors.

Billy's Reflections From the Field

In 2018, I attended the annual National Council of Teachers of English (NCTE) convention in Houston, Texas. An NCTE conference is an experience of thronging with thousands of fellow lovers of literacy, hearing from and meeting icons and leaders in the field, and feeling rejuvenated following the outpouring of inspiring stories and ideas.

While I attended sessions ranging from a few hundred to a few dozen participants, I was surprised to walk into my most anticipated session of the conference—an overview of the fourth edition of the *Handbook of Research on Teaching the English Language Arts* (edited by Diane Lapp and Douglas Fisher [2018])—to find only about a dozen attendees.

The handbook is jointly sponsored by NCTE and the International Literacy Association (ILA) and is published every six years or so, synthesizing and articulating the latest research findings related to the field of literacy. In this poorly attended session at the 2018 NCTE conference, Lapp and Fisher highlighted the latest research studies and their findings (Fisher, Lapp, & Whitmore, 2018). Yet, as the session wrapped up, Fisher curiously quipped, "You know, none of these research findings should surprise any of us . . . we've known what to do for at least the past three to four decades."

As participants gathered their bags and tapped on their phones, Fisher went on to lament that while the ideas about improving literacy continue to be consistent, one rarely finds entire systems (states or provinces, school districts, campuses) taking action. The theory isn't translating to wide-scale practice. I was a little bit stunned by the gravity of his thoughts; I knew they rang true. Looking around to see if anyone else felt slightly demoralized, I thought, "Hey, wait a second—we're trying!"

continued ▶

When the session ended, I walked up to Fisher and offered to drive him to the airport. I wanted to talk to him. I wanted to get his take on the literacy journey we were on in the secondary schools in the large Texas district I served. And I wanted to try to understand why research-based ideas weren't turning into action in literacy classrooms.

As we drove the thirty minutes or so to George Bush Intercontinental Airport, I shared my district's journey toward authentic literacy practices in secondary classrooms. I told the stories of investing in teacher expertise to move research-based ideas into action and then empowering teachers and students with inclusive, high-interest classroom libraries. Fisher listened and offered valuable advice, validation, and clarification.

This conversation, in my old blue Dodge, gave me hope. And hope is what we aim to offer you as you launch and continue your own journey into authentic literacy in your life, classroom, campus, school district, state or province, and nation. Moving ideas into action systematically is possible, if you have the courage, vulnerability, and self-awareness needed to navigate the pitfalls, errors, adjustments, and celebrations along the way.

This conversation also made me reflect on how applying what you learn and transferring it into new practice can be just as challenging for adults as it is for students. Reading research and understanding it doesn't mean you will turn the ideas into action; unfortunately, too often, this action doesn't happen. Beyond awareness of research, a lot of interpretation and negotiation needs to take place.

In fact, to apply and transfer research-based practices, teachers need prerequisites to application and transfer that greatly resemble those we lay out for students: meaningful relationships, open and frequent communication, interest and motivation, the ability to make choices, metacognition, a commitment to take risks and see errors as opportunities to learn, and ownership. Authentic literacy educators need to embrace and employ the same web of concepts and attitudes as students, if they hope to move ideas into action.

Some of the Ways Authentic Literacy Teachers Move Students From Thinking to Application

Thinking is a messy process and students often censure their own thinking because it can be a risk to put thoughts on display in front of peers and teachers. After all, anyone's thinking can be off-base or wrong at times. And who likes to be wrong in front of a crowd? Nevertheless, the goal of an authentic literacy teacher is to nudge students in the direction of confidently transferring learned skills to new contexts. The work of systematically drawing out student thinking must be a daily instructional habit—in other words, challenging students to sit with their errors and learn from them is an essential part of the authentic literacy classroom. Drawing out student thinking, even when the thinking may be wrong at times, is the first step for students to acknowledge and grapple with what they know and can do and what they don't know or can't do *yet.* Moving students from thinking to application and transfer of skills is intentional work and requires routine commitment from an authentic literacy teacher. To this end, an authentic literacy teacher takes the following actions.

- Identifies intrinsic motivation for each individual student
- Teaches students to read like writers using mentor texts and model texts

- Models inquiry processes by thinking aloud and demonstrating the writing process
- Explicitly defines the characteristics of authentic readers and writers to help students envision and move toward those identities
- Offers productive challenges that expand students' boundaries

The following sections detail each one. As you read, consider which ones you could incorporate into your own classroom. There is space to record your primary action steps in the "Your Turn" reproducible at the end of the chapter (page 87).

Identifying Intrinsic Motivation

How do you know when you have achieved intrinsic motivation with each individual student from your increasingly diverse population of learners? The first steps to answering this all-important question are maintaining a fundamental assumption that the answer is different for each learner, remembering the need for authentic relationships (see chapter 3, page 37), and ensuring that students are willing and able to make choices (see chapter 4, page 51). Graham (2018) writes, "Students develop as writers as a result of learning through deliberate agency" (p. 238). This means that students must be involved in making deliberate choices throughout the writing process—choices made in light of support from their teachers through direct instruction; exposure to a wide variety of texts, including from their independent reading; and useful tools and strategies at their disposal. Then what?

First of all, achieving intrinsic motivation is a reciprocal process, not an event. It naturally ebbs and flows with students' daily lives, dependent on the choices, feedback, and individual opportunities to extend learning that teachers provide to each student. Some students will be interested in and motivated by specific texts a teacher uses during direct instruction one week, and the next week, other students will be interested in and motivated by the texts the teacher uses then. While authentic literacy educators strive to motivate their unique and diverse students on an ongoing basis, at the same time, you must constantly look for evidence as the intrinsic motivation to learn and transfer skills becomes visible.

Intrinsic motivation becomes visible in students when the ideas they generate and work with during their learning are:

- Personal
- Relevant
- Interesting
- Meaningful
- Curious
- Impactful
- Attainable

In an authentic literacy class, you can functionally notice this taking place, or becoming visible, through the talk you encourage among the community of learners. And you can also concretely see it throughout the writing process. Writing, after all, is thinking explored and clarified on the page. And writing is the natural outcome of thinking and inquiry processes. As we pointed out in chapter 4 (page 51), writers write first to understand themselves and then to be understood by others. When students are intrinsically motivated to employ the writing process, they further their ideas and make connections to others. That's the type of outcome that helps teachers know when students are owning their learning.

Writers demonstrate application of skills based on their intrinsic motivation when they write letters to the editors of local news organizations about social and cultural issues that impact them, their peers, and their futures. Writers demonstrate intrinsic motivation when they write to local school boards and education policymakers about regulations that impact their learning environment. Time and time again, as intrinsic motivation takes hold, metacognition increases, and new learning is applied, students demonstrate authentic ownership of their literacy learning.

Teaching Students to Read Like Writers

When you consider reading, you likely think about readers comprehending and analyzing what they read, understanding the words, sentences, paragraphs, sections, and chapters—the textual characteristics that writers use to make meaning and share it with an audience. As readers begin to apply the skill of inquiry to their reading habits, their reading helps them "develop ideas for writing as well" (Graham, 2018, p. 246). This connection between reading and writing processes is one of the ways teachers ensure that their teaching practices are challenging, rigorous, and complex. And it is how learners begin to transfer critical literacy skills—applying what they learn as readers to what they demonstrate as writers.

Reading like writers helps students comprehend texts, see deeper themes and messages that authors share through their writing, and then, in turn, begin collecting ideas that they may want to explore throughout their own writing process and publications.

Questions you can pose to students as they read like writers include the following.

- What is the author saying about the world through this text?
- How does the author make connections with the readers?
- How does the author share messages and meaning throughout the text?
- What language does this author use to effectively create a noticeable tone?
- What are the specific techniques the author employs to affect the readers?
- How might you imitate or emulate specific techniques this author uses in your own writing?

Authentic literacy educators want students to see everything they read as a possible mentor for them as writers. When students begin viewing texts they read as potential mentors, they are reading like writers. They notice ideas, techniques, forms, structures, and more that they can then imitate in their own writing. The skill of reading like a writer to imitate the moves writers make and transfer them to one's own writing doesn't have to be limited by genre. For example, students can notice things writers accomplish in poetry to be applied in their own essays. On the other hand, model texts are an exemplar of the exact genre that teachers are asking students to write. For example, a model text for a persuasive essay would be an exemplar persuasive essay written by another writer. This is where we need to distinguish between mentor texts and model texts for writing.

Mentor Texts

Anything students read, view, or hear can mentor them as writers. This is the central idea of texts as mentors. Using texts as mentors helps teach students to read through a lens of inquiry, constantly asking themselves, "How did the writer do that? And what effect does that have on me, as a reader? And how can I learn from this writer to use language for an effect on my readers?" Inquiry isn't just about questioning the texts and authors one reads; it's about questioning oneself as a writer. Mentor texts facilitate this thinking and questioning process.

A byproduct of reading mentor texts like writers is that it helps students transfer what they know across literacy skills and genres, rather than seeing the skills and genres in isolation. You can help students transfer what they know about literary texts to argumentative and informational texts and back. You can help them see how writers of literary texts use rhetorical devices and how writers of argumentative and informational texts use figurative language.

We know there are certainly some writing characteristics that are specific to or more prevalent in certain genres, but good writers tend to use good writing techniques regardless of genre. Most characteristics specific to certain genres are related to structure (for example, stanzas in poetry). Helping students read like writers and recognize a text as a potential mentor allows them to suspend structure and focus on how writers make meaning. After all, both fiction and nonfiction texts help readers make sense of the world around them. Both are part narrative, part argument, and both have some amount of straightforward information to share with readers. The ideas and truths found in literary works are very real. And informational texts are not always true.

For far too long, educators have taught reading and writing as separate skills and processes—when they should be teaching them in an integrated fashion. And far too often, ELA classes teach genres in silos—more focused on how the genres are different from each other—when they should be teaching students the similarities based on what good writers employ. We further discuss mentor texts in chapter 7 (page 130).

Model Texts

While any text can be a mentor, a model text is an accomplished piece of writing, usually published, in the genre students are currently writing. Students study the text in order to improve their independent writing. Studying high-quality published essays while students are writing their own essays would be a good example of using texts as models. While students can learn about high-quality writing across genres (as mentioned in the previous section), using distinct genres for model texts is a good practice that helps students see an exemplar of the specific type of writing they are working to accomplish.

When using texts as models, students are still reading like writers. Students look at how the authors of the models accomplished specific effects so that they can form criteria that might guide their own writing. In the words of Graham (2018), "As students are introduced to new forms of writing or asked to create more sophisticated forms in a familiar genre, model texts provide examples of what is included" (p. 247).

While using texts as models for genres is useful, we have a word of caution: avoid allowing models to become formulas for writing. At times, well-intentioned teachers have fallen into the trap of providing students with model texts as an exact formula to follow. Why can this be problematic? All writers have unique strengths and challenges, and what may work for one writer will not necessarily work for others. It depends on the meaning each writer intends to create.

When giving students models, we recommend providing as many diverse examples as possible. For example, you could pull a set of model persuasive essays from the winners of the *New York Times* Student Editorial Contest. This way, students can study several different model essays by writers who have successfully crafted meaning through different means. The goal with models is to show students a variety of ways writing can work, not just one way.

Modeling Inquiry Processes

As we've mentioned throughout this book, modeling is essential to ensure authentic literacy practices. The same is true for provoking student inquiry and prompting students to own their thinking and learning.

You can engage students in thinking through their own interests, aspirations, curiosities, values, and beliefs if you first model yours by thinking aloud during instruction. Authentic literacy teachers think aloud as they interact with the ideas, messages, and meanings in the texts they read and beyond them into connected texts and topics—this is where authentic literacy teachers can evolve thinking to inquiry. They think aloud through the writing process as they explore ideas to write about and audiences to write for. Similarly, you can model your own reading interests and how reading interests are connected to personal interests and literary palates; in this way, you directly teach students how to discover and explore through writing the ideas and topics layered in their reading.

Authentic literacy teachers then pivot and model how writing ideas spring from a writer's life and experiences, including reading experiences. Teachers can explore, draft, and play with ideas to teach students how to think through ideas on the page and discover topics worth committing to and eventually publishing for an audience. Students then engage in inquiry of ideas in their own notebooks. This inquiry is by nature exploratory, low stakes, and often response driven based on ideas shared in class or found in texts all around the students—books, articles, poetry, media, and more.

After exploring ideas and audiences, teachers model how to transfer personal topics from writing form to writing form, with the opportunity for narratives to become arguments and arguments to become poems and poems to become college essays. And they model how a writer finds ways to publish those forms of writing with authentic audiences, seeking to influence, inspire, and even receive feedback for future ideas and inquiry, perhaps leading to the next book to read.

These aren't things that teachers can tell students to do. They are inquiry habits that influence reading and writing habits that can't simply be mandated or expected. If you want to ensure your readers and writers actually authentically adopt these habits, you must model what you expect—what it looks like, what it feels like—and you must do it over and over again.

Explicitly Defining Characteristics of Authentic Readers and Writers

While authentic literacy teachers model the type of thinking and inquiry students can do, they also explicitly describe the characteristics of real readers, writers, communicators, and thinkers in order for students to take ownership of these attributes. Teachers, collectively with students, create *anchor charts*. An anchor chart is a poster or other visual display, created collaboratively with students during the minilesson, that details significant points related to the topic or the skill being taught, which is then posted in the classroom for students to use as a guide as they practice applying the skill independently. Classes might create anchor charts that describe the following.

- How readers use their reading interests to expand and explore ideas discovered in the books they choose to read
- How writers use the ideas expressed in writing to expand and explore topics that lead to further meaningful inquiry and discovery
- How communicators learn how to convey ideas orally and in various forms of writing
- How thinkers learn how to integrate inquiry into literacy processes

Anchor charts like these help cement teaching points and typically remain visible in the classroom throughout a unit—they serve to remind students of the broad tenets of application of their learning. Essentially, anchor charts serve as reminders of the characteristics and habits of readers, writers, and communicators that students need to employ.

Offering Productive Challenges

As mentioned previously, taking risks and experiencing struggle and failure starts in one's thinking and decision making. Thus, authentic literacy teachers model risk taking, struggle, and even failure through their thinking and then in reading and writing. Taking calculated risks, struggling productively, and learning from failure are all essential elements that lead to growth as students transfer skills through application. However, teacher modeling is needed to ensure the following.

- The risks are calculated, and not just random.
- The struggle is productive, and not just painful.
- The failure is learned from, and not just experienced.

Productive struggle includes challenging students to read outside their comfort zones while continuing to support their thinking by providing daily opportunities to analyze, discuss, and imitate the sophisticated moves that proficient readers, writers, and thinkers make with a challenging text. To highlight and spark inquiry into challenging and sophisticated texts, authentic literacy teachers guide students in recognizing and evaluating the traits of literature that wins awards (such as Printz, Pulitzer, or National Book awards) while guiding students in determining their own criteria for literary acclaim.

Next, following student inquiry, teachers challenge student writers to try new genres and play with technique, style, and craft to reach new audiences. Authentic literacy teachers model these moves and provide students with opportunities to emulate the sophisticated moves that effective thinkers make in their writing. For example, you might do the following.

- Introduce students to and analyze different authors' writing processes and craft (for example, descriptions of J. K. Rowling's outline boards, Neil Gaiman's MasterClass lessons, and PBS NewsHour's book club's posts of authors' annotations of a chapter).
- Encourage students to collect quotes on writing from their favorite authors.
- Share authors' stories of how they became writers (for example, *Brave the Page* by Rebecca Stern and Grant Faulkner [2019]).

When it comes to speaking and listening, authentic literacy teachers engage students in activities that stretch their thinking, such as Socratic seminars, inner-outer circle discussions, fishbowl discussions, Harkness discussions, and other classroom discussion models. The goal is to provide students the opportunity to advocate, defend, and challenge ideas, including changing positions on their own ideas when evidence warrants it. Additionally, teachers can go beyond in-class discussions, such as connecting students with those in other classrooms—whether on the same campus or in other locations. Due to the experience of distance learning during the COVID-19 pandemic, teachers are better prepared to engage in digital discussions using Zoom and other virtual meeting software. Teachers can also use Flipgrid (an app that allows students to create short videos and collaborate with each other) and Twitter to connect to an even broader global community. For several years, Amy collaborated with a teacher in Russia, and students from both countries corresponded and crafted collaborative projects via Google Docs. Through digital technology and the internet, students connected with communities outside their direct experience, exposing them to new ideas, realities, and beliefs; challenging their worldviews; and developing empathy.

Summary

At the end of the day, authentic literacy educators strive to teach students how and why to mercilessly think through their own reading and writing processes. Inquiry is at the heart of it and is the engine of intrinsic motivation leading to the transfer of skills. You'll find that as you and your students develop deeply inquiring minds, considering the decisions made and the implications of those decisions, you'll be inspired to do it more. Student ownership and application will increase. Your authentic learning community members will excel as independent learners, and with great pride you'll witness growing excitement in your students for using literacy skills with most everything they do—and think—inside and outside the classroom.

Your Turn: Chapter 5

Reflecting on what you've learned in this chapter, record your primary action steps. As an authentic literacy teacher, I will:

-

-

In the novel *Cutting for Stone*, Abraham Verghese (2010) writes, "It is an axiom of motorcycling that you must always look in the direction you want to go and never at what you are trying to avoid" (p. 323). Think about the goals in this chapter that you are trying to accomplish with students and the things in your personal context that you may need to avoid. Respond to the following questions. Then, as you ask students to do, share your findings with a partner, colleague, or member of your team or book study group.

- Complete the phrase, "It is an axiom of authentic literacy that __________," and write about some of the big goals you must aspire to.

- What do you need to ultimately accomplish with your students in secondary literacy classrooms?

- What pitfall do you need to avoid in order to stay focused on what you need to accomplish?

CHAPTER 6

Feedback in the Authentic Literacy Classroom

Feedback builds on positive classroom relationships and guides students' progress toward authentic application of their literacy skills. Giving and receiving effective feedback requires *conversation*, a giving and taking (or at least consideration) of ideas, and a hard look at power dynamics in teachers' classrooms. Feedback in the authentic literacy classroom includes traditional teacher actions like commenting on student work and answering questions, but also promotes student voices, prioritizing them even. Teacher-to-student, student-to-student, and student-to-teacher interactions all present opportunities for giving and receiving feedback. In this chapter, we show how such interactions work, often interchangeably, in advancing student learning—the ultimate goal of effective feedback. We will share several practical strategies for authentic literacy feedback, but first, we address three essential facts about feedback: (1) that it starts with speaking and listening; (2) that it should *feed forward*, or provide information about what comes next; and (3) that its benefits outweigh its complexities.

Billy's Reflections From the Field

As part of my work as a district literacy leader, I often collaborate with teachers, visiting their classroom, to join them while conferring with students who are self-selecting books for independent reading and setting personal reading goals for the first time. During the early part of the fall semester of 2018, I visited a classroom and had the following conversation.

"Hi, Jessica. Tell me about what you're reading."

"Well, I'm currently reading *Jane Eyre* by Charlotte Brontë."

"That's a well-known classic with plenty of literary acclaim. Why did you choose it?"

"Honestly, my teacher just kept talking about what an amazing book it is and how it is one of the best classics."

"It sounds like you really value the recommendations your teacher makes. Did you set a personal goal for reading *Jane Eyre*?"

continued ▶

"Yes! My goal is to just enjoy it."

"Interesting; that's a great goal. How is it going?"

"If I'm being honest . . . terribly."

"Well, that's not good. What is terrible about it? You know, readers abandon books all the time . . . and that's OK! If you aren't enjoying *Jane Eyre*, you can always leave it behind and find something else to read. I do it all the time."

"No! That isn't the problem! I love the story so far!"

"What seems to be the problem, then?"

"It's frustrating! I sit down to read and find myself flying through the story, loving every moment, turning page after page, and then . . . I freak out and stop, worried that I'm not reading analytically enough, not taking enough notes, not marking places when Brontë uses literary devices. And then, without even realizing it, I find myself lost in the book again, turning page after page, loving every word, until I freak out again about not being analytical enough. It's terrible!"

"Wow, so, you're saying that it's going 'terribly' because you aren't able to achieve the goal you set for yourself—to 'just enjoy' reading *Jane Eyre*?"

"Exactly. But I really want to enjoy it. I just don't know how to stop worrying about what I'm missing if I don't slow down and take more analytical notes. I'm terrified that I'm messing up."

"Jessica, I want you to know that you don't need to take an analytical note over every little thing in this book to deeply understand and appreciate it. Writers intend for their books to wash over readers like waves. Sometimes, it's good to slow down and think deeply, but it's also good to just let the book pull you along in a rush of emotion and experience."

This conferring conversation proved valuable in a few different ways. First, I gathered data about the struggles Jessica encountered, which also served as a reminder to pay particular attention to advanced readers who may have similar challenges. Some students may be so used to having to analyze every book they read that they have difficulty just reading for pleasure. Second, conferring allowed me to provide personalized and immediate feedback to this student, based on the conversation. She quickly learned that I cared about her as a reader and that I understood her struggle, and I was able to reiterate the class goal of reading for enjoyment. Third, the conversation reminded me of the need to honor all titles when doing book talks: young adult titles, nonfiction titles, *and* the classics. Jessica chose to read *Jane Eyre* (Brontë, 1847/2017) because her teacher made it sound like a book worth reading.

Why Feedback Starts With Speaking and Listening

In a traditional secondary English classroom, speaking and listening often get short shrift. Students may stand at the front of the room, delivering presentations or reciting poems, while their peers take notes or evaluate performances. Teachers may facilitate Socratic seminars or ask students to do turn-and-talks about teacher-selected texts. Teachers ask questions and expect students to supply answers. It's not that these cannot be effective literacy practices, but we do suggest that these approaches are not the most valuable application of speaking and listening.

In the chapter of the *Handbook of Research on Teaching the English Language Arts* titled "Toward a New Appreciation of Speaking and Listening," we read:

> To speak/address the issue of speaking and listening is to acknowledge power dynamics and constructs that overtly, covertly, shape the dialogic relationship and inherent tensions between (a) speaker and listener, (b) teacher and student, (c) author and reader/viewer, and (d) language user and language learner. In this dialogic space, there is the negotiation of what counts as knowledge, whose voice is heard, and who gets to make such decisions—a space that ultimately involves power. (McLean, Prinsloo, Rowsell, & Bulfin, 2018, p. 120)

Teachers can examine the dialogic space within their classrooms by considering the following questions.

- Who is doing the talking? Who is doing the listening?
- Whose opinions are valued and validated?
- How are opinions valued and validated?
- Who gets to make decisions?

How teachers answer these questions is vital to their success as authentic literacy instructors. One cannot claim authentic reading, writing, and communicating practices unless the readers, writers, and communicators—every one of them—share in the power dynamics that make instruction possible. The previously referenced chapter continues:

> The act of engaged speaking and listening is central to critical literacy and pedagogy for it acknowledges the "Other," provides opportunities for students' authentic voice, and more importantly takes purposeful action in response to what was heard . . . power is only viable when it is applied, enacted, wielded. So, creating a space for students to share their perspectives is one thing; finding value in their voice, having their perspectives directly inform, disrupt, and transform the "next steps" and subsequent utterances is another. (McLean et al., 2018, p. 120)

Students "inform, disrupt, and transform the 'next steps'" by explaining their thinking, telling their teachers how they feel, sharing their goals and struggles, and informing their teachers of their needs as literacy learners. They make decisions that inform and drive instruction. This engaged listening and speaking *from student to teacher*, which includes visual cues like body language, is the most powerful form of feedback. In fact, Hattie and Clarke (2019) explain:

> The feedback teachers receive from students is our first and most important focus. The teaching/learning dynamic becomes synthesized when students are able to communicate their needs to teachers, and when teachers take account of everything in front of them which constitutes feedback from the student. (p. 90)

In an authentic literacy classroom, we call this engaged form of speaking with and listening to students *conferring*. Regular conferring is the routine that carries feedback as you help your learners grow in their identities as readers and writers. Simply put, *conferring* means having intentional conversations with students aloud or in writing, purposefully speaking *with* them as readers and as writers who can and should make decisions about their own work. Thus, this kind of interaction provides for teacher-to-student or student-to-teacher feedback, depending on individual student needs and a teacher's ability to be in tune with them. In conferring sessions, students should do most of the talking; therefore, the teacher's responsibility is to establish trust, ask open-ended questions, lean in, and listen. Sometimes the teacher might even repeat back what the student has said, and ask, "Can I help you with__________?" or "Would you like me to show you __________?" Instead of forcing a moment of private instruction that might compel a student's learning forward, the teacher asks what the student needs. This helps keep the balance of power in check and reminds students they own their reading and writing lives.

See "Thinking About Feedback" to reflect on effective feedback.

Reader Reflection: *Thinking About Feedback*

Think about your own work as you respond to the following questions.

- What kind of feedback makes you feel good about the work you've done?

- What kind of feedback makes you want to keep improving?

Visit ***go.SolutionTree.com/literacy*** *for a free reproducible version of this reflection.*

Why Feedback Should Feed Forward

Particularly in a literacy classroom, where skills acquisition requires practice, risk taking, and revision in order to ensure transfer, feedback must feed forward. *Feeding forward* means focusing on the future. No matter who is conferring with whom, whether it's a student reviewing goals with a teacher, two students helping each other edit their poems, or a teacher pointing out strengths and areas for growth in a student's recent composition, the following questions are valuable when helping learners improve: What can be changed? What solutions can be found? What steps can be taken?

In our experience, effective feedback must come while students are in the process of learning. And students are more apt to pay attention to teacher-to-student feedback when it has no grade attached; quite simply, "grades often tell the student 'the work is over'" (Hattie & Clarke, 2019, p. 2). If you've ever spent hours annotating students' papers just to have them ignore your feedback, you know this is true. Of course, students sometimes ignore feedback even without a grade, but this is less likely when they come to see feedback is important to their self-efficacy and growth. Ideally, teacher-to-student feedback should relate to the specific skills you teach during whole-class instruction or in conferences with individual learners so students can apply the feedback—that is, so they can feed it forward into their next steps.

Feedback that feeds forward creates possibilities that help students show improvement. It engages an "I can" attitude. And since trusting relationships provide a solid foundation, when teachers engage in teacher-to-student feedback opportunities, learners more readily take ownership. The teacher helps students, perhaps individually or in small groups, review what they've done, think about the process by which they've done it, imagine what they can do, and set goals for doing future work—in sum, helping readers and writers create road maps for their learning and ways to respond that show their growth.

Viewing feedback through this lens of possibilities has close ties to independent learning. As stated in *Teaching Literacy in the Visible Learning Classroom, Grades 6–12*:

> To ensure that students continue learning as they engage in tasks, assignments, or activities on their own, teachers must consider the tasks they ask students to complete. . . . Does [the task] promote metacognition? Does it promote goal setting? Does it promote self-regulation? (Fisher, Frey, & Hattie, 2017, p. 148)

The word *promote* here suggests forward motion—looking ahead toward what is to come. The feedback teachers seek as students read or write independently should also promote metacognition, goal setting, and self-regulation. Feedback that feeds forward promotes the same things. For example, consider the following prompts for eliciting student feedback that feeds forward, which illustrate the connection between assigned tasks and feedback in authentic literacy classrooms.

- Metacognition
    - Tell me what you're thinking.
    - Tell me about your process.
    - Tell me how you decided on ______________________________.
      (Fill in the blank with a book, topic, word, idea, and so on.)
    - Tell me the difference in this work from what you did before.
- Goal setting
    - What are you wanting to accomplish?
    - What's an idea you want to try?
    - When will you be able to do that?
- Self-regulation
    - How will you hold yourself accountable?
    - What steps will it take to do that?
    - What will you do if you get stuck?

Consider the value of the feedback students may provide as they learn to utilize questions such as these to become more engaged critical thinkers. With a keen focus on what students need to promote their own learning (namely, metacognition, goal setting, and self-regulation), authentic literacy teachers can help all learners come to appreciate feedback as a valuable asset, be it feedback students give teachers or feedback teachers give students.

See "Evaluating Assignments and Feedback" to analyze the relationship between your tasks or assignments and the feedback you have given your students.

Reader Reflection: *Evaluating Assignments and Feedback*

Think about the most recent tasks and assignments you've asked students to complete, and the feedback you provided to students at the completion of it. Then, complete the chart with as much detail about the feedback as possible.

Task or Assignment	Metacognition *Did your feedback promote metacognition? If so, describe how.*	Goal Setting *Did your feedback promote goal setting? If so, describe how.*	Self-Regulation *Did your feedback promote self-regulation? If so, describe how.*	Feed Forward *Did your feedback feed forward? If, so, describe how.*

Visit ***go.SolutionTree.com/literacy*** *for a free reproducible version of this reflection.*

Why Feedback's Benefits Outweigh the Complexities

We know working with adolescents can be a tricky business. As young people continue to grow and mature, their desire and ability to have authentic conversations may wax or wane. Motivations vary from student to student. Grades may motivate some students but not others. Some learners complete all assignments while others complete just a few. A few willingly revise their work to show new learning while others turn in first-draft thinking again and again. Accepting and acting on feedback can be complicated—for teachers and for learners—and you must expect and be prepared for the complexities that come with these vulnerable, human interactions.

Anyone who works with adolescents knows the importance of having thick skin and lots of patience. Some of the complexities these students bring with them, stir up, or make teachers guess at can seem unwieldy, and some teachers might shy away from conversations that bring discomfort. And sometimes teenagers react unexpectedly to questions or prompts. These behaviors are not unique to authentic literacy instruction. What might be new is the relationship and community, which can alleviate such reactions. When teachers establish relationships of trust with their learners (see chapter 3, page 37), and a community wherein all members trust one another, even "hard" conversations can produce positive results (Hattie & Clarke, 2019). Authentic literacy teachers must learn to read students, nudge them when necessary, and always respect their needs as thinking, feeling humans who are still learning to navigate life's uncertainties. When students trust that their teachers will give them honest and purposeful feedback, teachers have a better chance of helping learners make choices about their work when the feedback doesn't register quite right or students aren't in an emotional state to receive it.

Take for example a conferring session Amy had with a student we'll call Jordan. Jordan was already a strong writer when she started Amy's class, but she stayed in her comfort zone with her writing. She didn't experiment with structure, word choice, imagery, or any of the devices Amy taught in minilessons. Jordan was content to compose one draft and call it done, not interested in improving her craft. Every conferring interaction ended in disappointment for Amy because she knew if Jordan would invest in her writing, even a little, she'd grow from a strong writer and into an exceptionally talented one. Finally, Amy tried a different approach. She asked Jordan, "If you could write just one more piece and never write another thing again, what would you write that you'd be proud to put your name on?" Jordan shrugged like she usually did and offered little verbal feedback. Then, the next day, during independent writing time, Jordan called Amy over to her desk and shared an original poem—and it was breathtaking. In the conversation that followed, Jordan expressed that she'd always thought school writing was easy, and it bored her. She thought since they were writing essays, Amy wouldn't approve of her spending class time writing poetry. Amy realized that every previous conference had involved teacher-to-student feedback—Amy trying to give Jordan feedback that would help her want to improve her craft. But this conference, instigated by Jordan, opened Amy's eyes to the fact that Jordan had been giving Amy student-to-teacher feedback all along, and she'd ignored all of it simply because she was not in tune to Jordan's needs as a writer or how she felt about writing for school. The feedback

Jordan and Amy shared in that conference changed both of them. Amy learned to differentiate more effectively, and Jordan began applying her excellent poetic craft in her essays.

Learning students' needs and giving them space but at the same time giving them feedback that moves them forward can be a complex messiness. If you only focus on the positive, the things students do well, some students may not grow. If you only focus on the negative, the spots where learners struggle, some students will shut down. The authentic literacy expert finds ways to balance both because both are effective in moving students forward (Hattie & Clarke, 2019). While learners may initially balk at what they perceive as negative feedback, teachers can help them understand how "feedback thrives on errors and misconceptions" (Fisher et al., 2016, p. 23) because areas for growth and next steps may be easier to identify. As we discussed in chapter 5 (page 71), struggle and errors are essential parts of the learning process. With the focus on feeding forward, the teacher assists students in finding solutions, setting goals, and applying the skills that will lead to future successes.

Despite the complexities, feedback is beneficial and indeed necessary for authentic literacy learning. Here, we review four functions of feedback: (1) building relationships, (2) participating in the learning community, (3) gaining information that drives instruction, and (4) setting high expectations. When teachers engage in conversations with students, these four functions overlap, merge, and interact with one another.

Building Relationships

Conferring with students builds relationships and community, the importance of which we described in chapter 3 (page 37). Holding one-on-one informal conversations with students is especially important at the beginning of the school year as you work to quickly build authentic learning communities. These conversations can be spontaneous or planned, but they should be as nonthreatening as possible. Hattie and Clarke (2019) remind teachers, "The level of student self-efficacy affects the way in which [students] receive feedback" (p. 121). This is true at the beginning of the year and throughout it. Students' prior experiences in literacy courses may drive their attitudes when they enter the classroom, and teachers' first round of feedback should center on the idea, "I see you and want to know you as a person. How can I help?" Through these exchanges, not only do teachers get to know their students, but also students get to know their teachers. In the process, you establish routines for ongoing exchanges that move learning forward. These feedback opportunities may be scheduled conferences or interactions that pop up as a result of a need you see in class. Both contribute to individual student and community growth as readers, writers, and communicators.

Participating in the Learning Community

Feedback affords teachers an opportunity to model how authentic readers and writers communicate with one another. The speech you use matters. Do you use language that focuses on the reading and perhaps what the student does or doesn't understand, or do you use language that focuses on the reader and review or teach skills that validate his or her efforts and equip him or her with the ability to do better next time? Speaking with the intent to move learning forward can help you make better choices as you engage in giving and modeling feedback. Explicitly teaching students how to talk to one another as readers and writers is something you may want to consider as well. Remember the ultimate goal of authentic literacy instruction is to help students develop their identities as readers, writers, and communicators. You accomplish this in part by speaking to them as such—and then teaching them to speak to one another this way. As you practice this communication, you unite students as a community by modeling language that leads to learners' growing their identities, and thus their behaviors, as readers and writers. Authentic literacy educators establish a space of shared power where everyone's voice and perspective are valued and validated. They model the kind of talk and thinking students should use when engaging with teachers and each other in class (Hattie & Clarke, 2019).

Gaining Information That Drives Instruction

Collecting and correlating meaningful information that teachers can then use to design instruction is a critical function of feedback. When you tap into what students really think about their learning and what they really need in regard to skills acquisition, you can design instruction as a direct response to these thoughts and needs. Maybe you thought they understood a concept, but as you walk around the room, listening in on partner discussions as students work, you hear a lot of confusion about the task. This is a form of student-to-teacher feedback. So you stop, reteach, and model more. This is responsive teaching, and it's where the expertise of authentic literacy teachers can shine. Then, when you confer with individuals or small groups later, you can check for understanding and give feedback based on the needs students may still have. In addition, when you are wondering what content or skills you should teach next in a lesson cycle or unit plan, you can look to your learners, using the data you glean from all your feedback interactions. Where are learners' strengths? Where are their weaknesses? What might they have misinterpreted? and What scaffolding might they need? (Hattie & Clarke, 2019). Authentic literacy teachers, please remember: you teach learners, not content, and your readers, writers, and communicators can show and tell you what they need.

Setting High Expectations

Students respond to high expectations, and it's through genuine and honest feedback about their work that teachers communicate these expectations (Fisher et al., 2016). Through feedback interactions, teachers learn students' individual strengths and weaknesses and help them set high expectations for themselves. You link feedback to the learning objectives and to the appropriately challenging choices teachers guide students to make (Fisher et al., 2016)—choices they make based on what they determine to be their next steps. When teachers give specific, targeted feedback as a direct response to student needs and goals, students are more apt to respond to it. When you see students apply your feedback in their choices as readers and writers, you know your teacher-to-student feedback is effective, and students know their student-to-teacher feedback is effective when you shift instruction, reteach, differentiate, and adjust because of it.

See "Promoting Functioning Feedback" (page 98) to reflect on a few example feedback scenarios.

Reader Reflection: *Promoting Functioning Feedback*

The following scenarios offer opportunities for giving and receiving feedback, both student-to-teacher and teacher-to-student. Record and explain what you might do or say in each situation, keeping in mind that effective feedback should promote metacognition, goal setting, and self-regulation.

Several weeks into the new school year, you have a new student join your class. You've worked hard to develop relationships with your students, and they are all working well together in small groups and as a classroom community. You've established authentic literacy routines and set high expectations that include daily self-selected independent reading. How do you help this student become an authentic part of your learning community?

Students are working in pairs to give one another feedback on their writing. You overhear one student say to another, "I'm a better writer, so I'll just do it for you. It's too hard to explain." How do you help these students listen and speak to one another as writers?

You meet with a student who is reading a book you are surprised to find her reading. She tells you she chose this book because her friend suggested it, but when you ask her to tell you about what she's read, she has a hard time explaining any details, so you ask her to read you a paragraph. You find she is struggling with the language. How do you help this reader?

You read a student's most recent draft of an essay, and while the ideas are solid, you find that he hasn't incorporated any of the specific strategies or skills you've taught in the lessons. How do you help this writer?

Visit ***go.SolutionTree.com/literacy*** *for a free reproducible version of this reflection.*

Some of the Ways Authentic Literacy Teachers Get and Give Feedback

Opportunities for feedback present themselves in many ways in the authentic literacy classroom. In this section, we describe several strategies so you can visualize how giving and getting feedback in your own classroom for your own students might work.

To give and receive feedback, an authentic literacy teacher takes the following actions.

- Confers one-on-one with student readers and student writers
- Encourages informal communication among students
- Uses the language of feedback when helping students improve their work or develop future skills
- Keeps feedback records to ensure equity and track data

We address each one in the following sections. As you read, think about the actions you will try, and record your primary action steps in the "Your Turn" reproducible at the end of the chapter (page 107).

Conferring With Readers and Writers

Authentic literacy teachers routinely meet with students in one-on-one and small-group conferences. Conferring is a tool for gathering data; formatively assessing student thinking, reading, and writing; providing timely and actionable feedback to each learner; and receiving feedback from said learner. We recommend instilling this expectation at the beginning of the school year: "Students, I will be talking to you regularly about your reading life, the choices in books you make, and how you are working to grow as a reader. The same is true for your writing." Then, you must hold yourself accountable for doing so. Not only do these short conferring sessions help build and sustain relationships with students, but also they are an opportunity for teachers to receive feedback and help students make choices in regard to their learning. Talking face-to-face with learners gleans important information, and depending on the individual students' needs, you can recommend books, teach them specific skills, assess their learning, review their progress, celebrate their successes, and let them know they are seen, heard, and cared for as young humans.

The best times for conferring are during dedicated independent work times (see chapter 7, page 109). When students read self-selected books during dedicated reading time, teachers can confer with readers. When students write whatever they choose during dedicated writing time, teachers can confer with writers. Of course, providing feedback is not limited to only these dedicated work times, but establishing and maintaining these side-by-side routines ensure teachers have time to meet one-on-one with students and meet their individual needs.

Authentic literacy teachers have global questions and prompts that can spark meaningful conversations with learners, but teachers should personalize these conversations to the needs and strengths of each individual. Global questions might include the following.

- How's it going?
- What are you thinking?

- How can I help?
- What's going on with _____________? (Fill in the blank with a character in the book the student is reading, the topic of the first draft of an essay the student is writing, and so on.)

There are also a variety of prompts and sentence frames that teachers can use to give feedback. These strategies work well as guides for verbal feedback and for written feedback. These strategies are also easy to teach students, so they can effectively give one another feedback in partnerships or small groups. One option is the *2–2–1* strategy, which involves stating two positive comments, two questions, and one pro tip, as follows.

- **Two positives:** Identify places within a student's work where he or she (a) has applied a skill learned through class instruction or (b) has exceeded expectations. For example—
    - "This word choice in this sentence packs a punch, and that makes me want to know more."
    - "What a unique and clever comparison!"
- **Two questions:** Draw attention to places within a student's work where he or she (a) could have applied a skill learned through class instruction or (b) could improve when revising. For example—
    - "How might using imagery make this description more vivid?"
    - "Would this be a good place for some specific examples?"
- **One pro tip:** As the authentic literacy professional, you are the expert on what will prompt a student in the right direction. The pro tip might serve to help a student feel seen or heard, or it could be a bit of feedback that reminds a writer to take a little more time with his or her work. There's no clear guideline here; trust yourself as the pro! For example—
    - "Remember, punctuation is important to the meaning you create. Try not to confuse your reader by not using any! ☺"

Another excellent strategy is *I wonder, and I think*. This simply involves starting each comment with the words *I wonder* as a way to engage in possibilities with readers and writers. Then, give them a starting place to *think* about. Consider the following examples.

- "*I wonder* what you thought as you read this paragraph. *Think* about how you might note your thinking as you read."
- "*I wonder* what the theme of this piece is. *Think* about marking the text with key words or phrases that might help you link big ideas together."
- "*I wonder* what tone you are trying to create in this piece. *Think* about using more specific word choice."
- "*I wonder* what adding some sentence variety would do for your rhythm. *Think* about adding some short sentences along with your long ones."

The goal is for the student to lead the conversation as much as possible, taking ownership of his or her thinking and learning as student-to-teacher feedback informs the instructional moves teachers make in response to student learning. Students use their reading and writing lives, including written entries in their reader-writer notebooks (see chapter 7, page 118), as evidence of their thinking and progression in reading and writing skills during formal and informal conversations with teachers.

Conferring in its simplest form is a conversation, but when practiced intentionally, with a focus on feedback that feeds forward, it becomes sophisticated teaching and data collection, and it requires sophisticated listening skills.

As an example, consider this interaction from Amy's classroom. Students were on their third day of drafting op-ed essays. Prior to starting to write, students had already read, discussed, and studied five different model texts by various writers with a specific focus on the moves the writers made to create meaning. They had chosen their topics and were supposed to be close to completing their first full draft.

> *"How's it going, Elayna?" Amy asked a student during a one-on-one conference.*
>
> *"Don't ask."*
>
> *"That good, huh? What's the trouble?"*
>
> *"I don't know where to start."*
>
> *"But you told me some fantastic ideas when we talked about your topic last week. What happened?"*
>
> *"I just don't know where to start."*
>
> *"You mean, like, the first sentence? Or the whole introduction? Or what?"*
>
> *"All of it. I don't know how to get the ideas going."*
>
> *"What have you written so far?"*
>
> *"Nothing."*
>
> *"OK, so how about we pull out those pieces we read in class—you know, the texts we are learning from for this essay? Let's look at those again and see how those writers start." While Elayna rummaged in her backpack, Amy reminded her that it's OK to start anywhere when writing—it's OK to go back and work on an introduction after having written out one's main ideas. Elayna said she couldn't write that way. She retrieved the handouts and spread them out on her desk.*
>
> *"Let's look at each of the openers in these essays," Amy said. "Just read them and see if you can define what each writer does. Remember the lesson we had on ledes? Writers begin their writing in different ways. They might start with anecdotes, or explanations, or even a list of facts. What do you see these writers do?"*
>
> *"This one tells of something that happened in the news, and so does this one, and this one. They all do."*
>
> *"Hmm. Interesting, right? Why do you think all these writers do that?"*
>
> *"Because it's interesting? Because it's something they care about?"*

> *"You're remembering things we've talked about now, right? I know you've got a story—that's how you decided on a topic. I bet you can write that story as your intro."*

This example shows a student who mostly just needed encouragement and a reminder that she had learned how to write an introduction to her essay. Nudging her to return to the mentor texts proved useful too; she kept the papers on her desk throughout the week to look at as she drafted. This student writer showed she understood the value of studying proven writers to get ideas for writing—something all good writers do. This conversation also reminded the teacher (Amy) to more quickly move around the room and check in on every student—this student had spent two full days pretending she was working. Finally, this conferring highlighted for Amy that all the mentor texts used a similar opening. While that worked out in this case, she thought perhaps a wider variety would be better for next time.

This example reiterates the importance of *student-to-teacher* feedback. There's valuable information to gain for improving instruction, not just for the individual student you confer with but for *all your students*. If one student struggles with an idea, a concept, or a process, you can be confident others do as well. This feedback shines a light on what you might need to reteach, what reminders you might need to give, and even how you might better unite the community. The insights teachers gain from listening as students talk about their thinking and their learning experiences are invaluable in the process of helping the students grow as independent thinkers, confident readers, and accomplished writers.

See "Determining Whether It's Time for a Conversation" to reflect on your students and your conferring practice.

Reader Reflection: *Determining Whether It's Time for a Conversation*

Note: This activity assumes you've been in class with a set of students long enough to know their names. If that's not the case for you right now, come back to this later.

Choose one of your class periods for this exercise. Then, close your eyes and imagine the students in this class. Make a list of all their names.

Next, compare your list with your class roster. Did you remember everyone? If not, perhaps it's been a while since you met with certain students one-on-one, and it's time to do so.

Next, make a note next to each student's name, detailing any or all of the following: (a) something personal you know about the student, (b) a reading or writing goal the student is working toward, or (c) a book title you think the student might enjoy.

Source: Adapted from P. Kittle, personal communication, July 2014.

Visit ***go.SolutionTree.com/literacy*** *for a free reproducible version of this reflection.*

Encouraging Student-to-Student Communication

Authentic literacy teachers invite and encourage speaking and listening in many contexts—not just for conferring. Authentic literacy teachers know adolescents are social by nature, and they know to take advantage of students' need to communicate with one another. Talk is an important and empowering element in an authentic literacy classroom. Ask students to turn and talk to one another about their thinking around a text or concept. Ask them to read aloud the writing they've composed in their notebooks. Ask them to engage in small-group or whole-class conversations around a text.

Remember, authentic readers and writers talk to others about their reading and writing. This talk can be as unstructured as having students chat about a book in self-selected small groups or as structured as assigning small groups of students who meet to workshop their writing. For more structured talk, be sure to teach students how to give feedback that feeds forward. The following strategies can be helpful in establishing productive speaking and listening protocols in the classroom.

- Discuss with students their preferences for shared talk around reading and writing. Record their responses and consider turning these responses into a classroom poster.
- Facilitate a silent discussion on what makes for good speaking and listening by giving students sticky notes to record their ideas. Create a T-chart with one column labeled "Speakers Should" and the other labeled "Listeners Should" and post it on a wall in the classroom. Invite students to stick their ideas in the appropriate columns.
- Provide "talk and respond" sentence stems to help students discuss their reading and writing. For example, for discussing self-selected independent reading books:
    - Talk—"What is interesting about __________ [the characters, conflict, plot, and so on]?"
    - Respond—"I hear what you're saying about __________. This makes me think of __________."

  When discussing a piece of writing, students might say:
    - Talk—"Do you think my __________ [hook, thesis, metaphor, transition, and so on] is effective?"
    - Respond—"When I read that part, I thought __________, which helped me __________."

  In these examples, notice how specific talking points—related to specific reading and writing skills—will make a difference in the quality of student talk. Teaching students how to talk about specifics preempts surface-level and short, yes-or-no conversations.

Directly and through modeling, guide students to use the language of feedback (covered in more detail in the next section, page 104), just as teachers do. Of course, using this language takes practice. That's OK. Practicing productive talk is a valuable use of instructional time and allows authentic literacy teachers to lean in and listen and receive feedback.

Traditionally, a classroom with this much talk might seem out of control. We maintain that a talkative class can certainly be a productive one. That's not to say it's a breeze keeping every student on task—classroom culture is key to making authentic literacy instruction work, and with high expectations for all learners, teachers continually build this culture through the routines they employ within each class period. All along, authentic literacy educators model how to listen respectfully and how to respond appropriately—this is part of establishing a community of like-minded learners.

Using the Language of Feedback With Readers and Writers

Effective feedback begins and ends with the language used to convey it. With authentic literacy, language choices are especially important because you are teaching readers and writers, *not* teaching reading and writing. The ultimate goal is to help learners develop their identities and take on the characteristics of those who think, talk, and act like real readers and writers—not those who just read and write for school. After all, it is *who* you are teaching, the students, not *what* that matters. Authentic literacy teachers must view students as individual humans, readers, writers, and communicators first—a significant starting point that dictates any content or necessary reading, writing, or communication skills that should follow in the learning process.

Therefore, the language authentic literacy teachers use in class—particularly when conferring with students—must reflect the focus on students' identities and their right to make choices. When you use language that strengthens these identities, it empowers students' sense of agency as they make choices about what and how they read and what and how they write (Fisher et al., 2016). The following examples are prompts and questions that empower readers and writers.

Language that focuses on the reader includes:

- Tell me what you thought as you read this text.
- What line resonated with you the most? Why?
- Was there anything that confused you?
- How did __________ make you feel?
- Why do you think the author described that in this way?
- What does this text remind you of?
- Would you recommend this text to someone else? Why or why not?
- How can I help?

Language that focuses on the writer includes:

- Tell me what you thought as you wrote this.
- What line resonates with you the most? Why do you like the way you wrote it?
- How did you decide on your topic, form, or structure?
- What are you hoping to accomplish with this word choice?
- What do you think would help the sentences flow more smoothly?
- How do you think your audience will feel when they read this?
- How can I help?

The student is at the heart of authentic literacy practices, and he or she makes choices. The teacher's aim should be to help him or her grow and use agency to become a more accomplished reader and writer. Teachers can best accomplish this by using language that empowers the student.

Amy's Reflections From the Field

After handing back students' best drafts of spoken-word poems with written feedback that focused on the skills students had learned in minilessons—some of the feedback positive but most of it written with a hope students would want to do better—I approached one of my students to hold a quick conference because I hadn't met with him in a while.

"Hey, Conrad, tell me what you're thinking."

"I'm thinking I'm a terrible writer."

"That's not what I think. I read your poem, and you've got some punch-in-the-gut lines there."

"But you said I needed to change so much. I let my friends read my poem, and they thought it was great. Now, I think I'm not as good at all this as I thought I was. I just don't know what you want."

"Oh, I've really messed up if I've made you think that. I am sorry. I only intended to give you ideas you might want to play around with as you revise. Some writers need that prompting, but it's *your* writing. You decide what works for the meaning you are trying to make."

"So what will my grade be if I just leave it as is?"

I learned important things about what Conrad might need from me in this short exchange. I already knew he was a competent writer because I'd read his previous work, but I doubted he pushed himself very hard to get any better at his craft. He pretty much confirmed my suspicion when he so quickly jumped to the question about grades. (I didn't answer him, by the way. I did encourage him to play with some different word choice since he had a whole class period to make revisions.) Conrad reminded me that not all student writers interpret teacher feedback the same way. He thought I was being critical of what he'd written, which was not the case. I realized I hadn't balanced my feedback, which was something I needed to keep in mind for all my students. This writer needed more positives in order to boost his confidence, and he needed to know he owned the writing, not me. Giving Conrad feedback to help him grow wasn't about what I wanted—it was about him making choices as a writer.

Keeping Feedback Records

Keeping records of the conversations you have with learners is an important element of giving and receiving effective feedback. For any data to be useful, whether they concern instruction as a whole or individual students, keeping records is vital. We have tried keeping records in multiple ways: printing templates with boxes for specific data, using note-taking apps, stacking printer paper on clipboards, and labeling pages in spiral notebooks with students' names. They all work just fine. We do not think there is a one-size-fits-all record-keeping strategy, but we do think there are essential data that teachers should record to best utilize feedback. These data include the following.

- Which student did I talk to?
- When did we talk?
- What did we talk about?
- What struggles and successes did we discuss specifically in relation to the student's learning?
- What are the student's goals moving forward?

Then, teachers use the information collected to inform next steps in their instruction.

A final note about record keeping: from our experience and observations, it's often the quiet student—the one who does his or her work, keeps mostly to him- or herself or to a small group of friends, and seemingly understands the lessons taught—who gets the least one-on-one talk time with the teacher. On the other hand, it's the rambunctious student, the one who may need redirection or reminders of established routines and who seemingly doesn't understand the lessons, who gets the most one-on-one talk time with the teacher. Teachers often spend most of their time and energy with the off-task student, leaving little for everyone else. Keeping accurate records of every feedback interaction can help teachers alleviate this disparity, so all students have adequate, if not equitable, opportunities for feedback.

Summary

We started this chapter with the need for authentic conversation—practiced speaking and listening—in order to shift the power dynamics within a classroom. What followed is a palette of ideas from which you can pick and choose as you grow in your expertise working with adolescent learners. To become effective as an authentic literacy teacher who knows how to get and give feedback, start with one aspect of this chapter related to getting your students talking, and then—with extreme attention to listening—model and mold your students' talk into effective feedback. What resonates with you regarding student conversations? What seems easy enough to implement immediately? What piqued your intrinsic motivation to do more with conferring in your classroom? The answers to these questions are the most important things you can put into action, ensuring that feedback always feeds student learning forward.

Then, as you get comfortable with one facet of effective feedback, come back to this chapter and add another layer. Meanwhile, no matter what you choose to do, simply talk with secondary students as the emerging adults they are. Listen to what they say and how they say it. Notice their nonverbal communication. Lean in and listen with intention. As you practice functional and effective student-to-teacher and teacher-to-student feedback, the things you need to know in order to effectively influence students' literacy skills will be revealed to you. They might be revealed in whispers as you kneel beside a student's desk, or they might come shouting with calls for help across the classroom, but as you focus on instilling skills in listeners and speakers the way you do in your readers and writers, they will come, and your students will be even more prepared for the literacy lives they will lead beyond secondary school.

Your Turn: Chapter 6

Reflecting on what you've learned in this chapter, record your primary action steps. As an authentic literacy teacher, I will:

-

-

The art of giving and receiving feedback is essentially about the art of effective communication. Tony Robbins (2008), a well-known life and business strategist, has stated, "To effectively communicate, we must realize that we are all different in the way we perceive the world and use this understanding as a guide to our communication with others" (p. 237). Think about that statement as it relates to the content of this chapter and the students you teach. Then, choose one of the following prompts, and write a response. Share your writing with a trusted peer or colleague, or perhaps in your book study group; then, ***ask for feedback***. Note the language your partner or your group members use and how it makes you feel.

- To give oral feedback with fidelity, teachers must establish a classroom culture where all learners adhere to routines that allow for teachers to confer with individual readers and writers. Write a script that details how you will share and model this information with your students.

- Think about the value of talk as it relates to learning. Write an original poem or reflective piece that illustrates one experience you've had where communication aided, interfered with, or created learning.

CHAPTER 7

Classroom Routines That Build Authentic Reading and Writing Habits

We began this book with a call for secondary literacy educators to embrace authentic literacy practices in the classroom. In this final chapter, we draw all the moving parts together and illustrate how teachers can implement authentic literacy routines that develop the habits of mind of authentic readers and writers. Authentic literacy instruction is not just an idea or mindset but a methodical daily practice. By outlining these routines, we hope that all educators can see a pathway forward to transforming their classroom in the best interest of all learners.

This transformation begins to take shape when students are at the center of learning. You can determine whether students are at the center when you answer a few simple yet purposeful questions.

- Who makes the choices about what to read and what to write?
- Who does the majority of the talking?
- How is this talk used to develop literacy skills, provide feedback, and adjust or modify curriculum and instruction?
- How do relationships and community facilitate learning?
- How does individual application of literacy skills become habit?

Your answers to these questions may expedite your need to align beliefs with practice, especially as it relates to authentic literacy instruction. Establishing daily routines in ELA classes can help speed up the transformation and provide a means of sustaining it. Since the overarching goal is to help students develop their identities as readers and writers who read and write beyond school, teachers must establish the routines in school that will help them do so. In classrooms dedicated to authentic literacy, teachers implement and foster routines intent on engaging students in relevant and meaningful reading, writing, listening, speaking, and thinking tasks that grow their individual capacities in authentic and experiential ways—and teachers and students do these things almost every day.

We say *almost* every day because education is filled with exceptions and adjustments. The moment we say *every* day, we've created an expectation that isn't fully achievable. Would these routines be valuable and effective every day? Of course! However, bell schedules change, fire drills happen, and high-stakes testing doesn't seem to be going away anytime soon. In reality, striving for these instructional routines to occur almost every day in secondary ELA classrooms is an attainable goal for every literacy teacher.

The instructional routines we outline in this chapter are meant to be flexible, not rigid and formulaic. When you put them into action to the best of your ability, you will see immediate ways to be responsive to the unique needs of your learners. To be clear, these instructional routines should not be understood or deployed in isolation; they are all related, integrated, and complementary of one another.

Daily authentic literacy routines are the vehicle for all the components of authentic instruction that motivate students to identify as readers and writers; in fact, these routines incorporate what Guthrie and Wigfield (2018) call the "big five" motivation processes (p. 58): they leverage *intrinsic motivation* and *social* interaction, foster *self-efficacy*, and employ ideas that learners find relevant and *valuable* to increase *engagement*. In the remainder of this chapter, we describe these routines and provide applicable guidance for implementing them.

Amy's Reflections From the Field

Another student said, "I don't know." And another. And another.

It was day three of my making the rounds in my senior English class, leaning in to quietly chat with readers during our devoted independent reading time. They had selected books a few days earlier, and I was checking in, making conferring an ongoing routine. I could talk to five or six students in this fifteen minutes. "What do you think?" I asked, nodding to the book open in their hands. Most mumbled, "I don't know," until I prompted for more, and then I got answers like "It's OK." A couple said, "I really like it."

I wasn't new to self-selected independent reading. I had started making space for it in my instructional routines over a decade before, when I first realized many of my high school students read far below grade level. I *was* new to having to work so hard to get students to talk to me about their books. I realized pretty quickly most didn't know how.

The next period, I changed my question, thinking I would work on knowing my readers more and ease into getting them to share their thinking. "What's the best book you've ever read?" I asked. "You know, your favorite?"

Most shrugged and said, "I don't know." A couple said, "I can't remember." One said, "I'm not really a reader." Not one could name a title—or an author—of a book they loved.

By midday, I'd met with seventeen students, all close to graduating high school, none able to talk to me about a book they were currently reading or one they'd read and liked in the past.

Then, in my last period of the day, I knelt next to Miranda. Before I could even ask my question, she asked me one. "Can I tell you about a book I read this summer?" she said, taking me by surprise. "I think parents should have to read this book."

Miranda went on to tell me how the conflict in the book related to her life, how one of the minor characters was so much like her, and that if her parents would read it, maybe they would understand what she was going through; maybe they would stop yelling at her, grounding her, and making her so sad. Maybe they could get along again.

I don't remember the book. Or the author. I do remember the look in Miranda's eyes as she pulled the book from her backpack, shoved it in my hands so I could see the book she talked about so passionately, and shared heartfelt thoughts about her life and her reading.

I learned a lot about Miranda in those few minutes, and she validated what I already knew about the importance of books: they can help people feel less alone, see into the lived experiences of others, and think about their lives.

I want that for all my students. That's why every day, we read the books we choose for ourselves, and every day, I visit with a few students about what they're reading and what they think. And one day, maybe, every student will find a favorite and no longer cling to "I don't know."

Authentic Literacy Instructional Routines

Before we discuss specific literacy routines, think back to the introduction (page 1), where we referred to Fisher and his colleagues' (2016) reminder that teachers have choices to make about what to leave behind as they craft instruction that centers on students and their identities as readers and writers. Authentic literacy instruction requires the use of texts, tools, and strategies authentic to real readers and writers, not those who just read and write for school. While the focus in this approach is on the *who*, "*What* and *when* are equally important when it comes to instruction that has an impact on learning" (Fisher et al., 2016, p. 21). Authentic literacy teachers practice the *what* by implementing routines that lend themselves to habit formation. *When* includes following pacing guides that align with skills-based standards, and being responsive to the individual needs of learners—daily, weekly, monthly, and yearly because students and students' needs change.

Establishing effective routines begins with ensuring learners know the expectations. When authentic literacy teachers build community, they establish the expectation that all students will work to develop their identities as readers, writers, and communicators. That's the overarching, all-important target. Students learn more when expectations for their learning are clear, so tell them directly (Fisher et al., 2016). Environments wherein teachers establish routines embed and remind students of expectations in consistent and challenging ways. When your students know the end goal is to help them develop their identities as readers, writers, and communicators, it provides context and purpose for the daily goal of practicing what readers, writers, and communicators do.

Authentic literacy teachers work to ensure learners know the tasks they are asked to do are worthwhile. Further, they help students see that these tasks will allow them to recognize their growth as they become increasingly independent, which then leads to further motivation to take risks, accept challenge, and improve. Therefore, the literacy teacher's first responsibility in regard to preparation includes setting up systems and routines focused on the following three goals (Fisher et al., 2016).

1. Challenging, stretching, and growing students' thinking and skills acquisition
2. Promoting students' self-efficacy and self-awareness
3. Defining what the teacher wants students to learn and do and what it looks and feels like when students are successful

These broad aims may seem distant or difficult to achieve, so we provide features to help you visualize how to accomplish them. These features promote habits of mind, personal ways to learn, and clear expectations for readers and writers, an imperative for learning: "Teacher clarity about learning expectations, including the ways in which students can demonstrate their understanding, is powerful" (Fisher et al., 2016, p. 27). Not only do you want powerful learning, you want to empower students as they take on the responsibility for their own growth. To move students toward ownership, authentic literacy practitioners meet students where they are and purposefully strive to ensure all students have the following.

- Access to books they want to read and time in class to read them
- Clarity about what they're learning, why they're learning it, and how they're learning it
- Appropriate tools to explore learning and thinking as readers and writers
- Space in a sharing, safe, collaborative classroom community
- Ongoing feedback to propel their learning forward
- Resources to prompt, provoke, challenge, and guide them as readers and writers

Consider how your current practice reflects these features with "Ensuring Daily Features of the Authentic Literacy Classroom."

Reader Reflection: *Ensuring Daily Features of the Authentic Literacy Classroom*

Intrinsically, all literacy teachers know some of the ways to meet the needs of students and engage them in healthy, growth-producing relationships and learning. Think about the following instructional features and reflect on how you currently ensure all students have access to each one.

- My students have access to books they want to read and time in class to read them.

- My students have clarity about what they're learning, why they're learning it, and how they're learning it.

- My students have appropriate tools to explore learning and thinking as readers and writers.

- My students have space in a sharing, safe, collaborative classroom community.

- My students receive ongoing feedback on their learning.

- My students have resources, such as a wide variety of texts, that mentor and challenge them as readers and writers.

Visit ***go.SolutionTree.com/literacy*** *for a free reproducible version of this reflection.*

Some of the Ways Authentic Literacy Teachers Establish Reading and Writing Routines

So far in this chapter, we've outlined broad aims for motivated student learning and the general features educators need to implement so that all students stretch, take risks, and grow into their potential as readers and writers. Now, let's get into even more specifics about what these features look like in authentic literacy classrooms.

When implemented with fidelity, the following instructional routines will help you accomplish your goals as an authentic literacy teacher. You will be able to teach to students' lived experiences, spark and sustain their intrinsic motivations, establish and maintain relationships, and develop a community wherein identifying and growing as readers, writers, and communicators becomes the cultural norm. For each of these routines, we provide an explanation of why it matters to student learning and a description of how these routines interact with and complement one another. Each section includes specific actions teachers and students must take to achieve deep, sustained implementation. Please remember: these routines work best in alliance, purposefully moving learning forward.

An authentic literacy teacher employs the following instructional routines as students actively participate.

- Self-selected independent reading
- Independent writing
- Conferring
- Using reader-writer notebooks
- Teaching via skills-based minilessons
- Thinking aloud
- Collaborating
- Using mentor texts

Read the following sections closely and record your primary action steps in the "Your Turn" reproducible at the end of the chapter (page 133).

Self-Selected Independent Reading

Dedicated daily reading time in class builds students' habits for a reading life outside of class and allows teachers to guide students in the processes in which real readers engage, for both personal and analytical purposes. We refer to this practice as *self-selected independent reading* (SSIR) to emphasize that students choose what they want to read and do so individually. Student choice in reading leverages interest and intrinsic motivation, building volume and endurance as students read increasingly complex texts across genres. Teachers support student choice and challenge and guide students to select books and genres outside their comfort zones. Independent reading provides an avenue for students to explore complex themes, acquire new vocabulary, experiment with sophisticated sentence structures, notice nuanced text features, and engage with cognitively demanding content and subtle relationships among ideas. This practice builds the identity and stamina of readers (Kittle, 2013). Supported by regular conferring (page 117) and purposeful instruction (individually when warranted, along with whole-class skills-based minilessons, page 119), it accelerates acquisition of language skills and develops high levels of social and academic language proficiency.

Self-selected independent reading, as we define it, is not the same as initiatives like Sustained Silent Reading (SSR) or Drop Everything and Read (DEAR). While SSR and DEAR focus solely on time to read, self-selected independent reading is an instructional routine. It builds a framework for intrinsically motivated readers to apply critical literacy skills in response to direct instruction. For example, say we teach plot structures. Our students can apply this instruction by creating a storyboard of whichever book, fiction or literary nonfiction, they may have chosen to read. Self-selected independent reading also requires more interaction between teachers and students than other initiatives. It intertwines with conferring, allowing the teacher to receive and give feedback. During self-selected independent reading, you meet with your readers in short sessions—sometimes chatting about their books, or helping them find books they want to read, or checking for understanding, or assessing skills. The feedback received while you confer during self-selected independent reading time is critical evidence of student learning needs that influence future minilessons (see page 119).

While giving instructional time to self-selected independent reading may seem like a huge investment, consider the payout. Self-selected independent reading as a daily instructional routine builds a sense of ownership, relevance, engagement, and personal and social value—all contributing to intrinsic motivation and authentic learning for every student.

You will find the time because you believe in the impact of students' making choices about their learning, and you know the only way for students to develop reading identities is to read. Authentic literacy teachers promote self-selected independent reading by routinely providing time and space for it and providing a robust classroom library of high-interest, relevant books within students' easy reach (see chapter 4, page 55).

Depending on the length of your class periods, we recommend devoting ten to fifteen minutes per day to this essential habit-building routine. Often, self-selected independent reading occurs at the beginning of class. This helps students quiet their minds when they enter the classroom, reinforces reading as a daily habit, and allows the teacher time and space to conduct administrative business such as setting up the minilesson, taking attendance, and perhaps conferring with a student who's been absent. However, self-selected independent reading can also occur after the minilesson to facilitate students' collaborative and independent application of literacy skills with the books they have chosen to read.

Of course, class time is not the only time we hope students will read. Ideally, students also read their self-selected books outside of class as part of their own daily routines and at home. However, in reality, many students may never give books a chance outside of class if they do not have the opportunity and time to explore books and read for even short bursts of time with peers and teachers to encourage them. As Daniel T. Willingham (2015) suggests in the article "For the Love of Reading," with dedicated class time for independent reading, teachers have a chance to change student beliefs—"beliefs about what is worthy of sustained attention and what brings rewarding experiences." Every reader we know believes in the rewarding experience of reading, and every young person you inspire to open a book can know this, too.

To implement and sustain the routine of self-selected independent reading, teachers and students must be active participants. Setting the expectation that all students read books of their choice, try to apply skills-based lessons to their independent reading, and ultimately develop a habit of reading is a prerequisite for implementation, as is students' knowing the teacher will confer with them about their reading lives. Table 7.1 (page 116) shows teacher and student actions that foster a habit of self-selected independent reading. Remember, the goal of authentic literacy instruction is to have students graduate as lifelong readers. Meeting this goal requires concerted, intentional effort and time to practice reading with an authentic literacy expert.

Independent Writing

Reading and writing are inextricably linked. Yet when it comes to time devoted to literacy instruction, writing is often a much smaller piece of the pie. Just as authentic literacy teachers devote class time to self-selected independent reading, they must give students time for independent writing. The essential ingredient to shift the culture of writing instruction is time—time for students to build experience with writing, and time for students to write from authentic, relevant, and personally meaningful experiences (Graham, 2018). Students are not bad writers and good writers—there are only writers who have had more experience with writing and writers who have had less experience with writing.

Table 7.1: Self-Selected Independent Reading—Activators for Deep Routine Implementation

Teacher Actions	Student Actions
• Talking about books that will engage readers • Surveying the room, reinforcing the expectation for silent independent reading; redirecting as needed • Conferring with students about their independent reading or helping them find a new book to read • Taking notes about feedback received from students during conferring	• Noting books or authors they might want to read or explore • Reading independently • Holding peers accountable for quiet reading time once a community of trust is established • Conferring with the teacher about their independent reading or efforts to find a new book to read

Just as self-selected independent reading develops student readers' identities and habits of mind, independent writing does so for student writers. All writers write more than they will ever let anyone read. They keep notebooks where they store ideas, jot down descriptions, practice with style, and collect quotes or interesting vocabulary. Sometimes independent writing might look like personal or text-based response writing (pages 63 and 64). Sometimes independent writing might look like thirty heads bent over notebook paper or laptops as students compose pieces they intend to publish as assignments. And just like you confer with students during self-selected independent reading time, you confer during independent writing time, especially when students are in the process of generating ideas or refining their style, not just playing with language in their notebooks while writing low-stakes responses. However, use caution when interrupting writers when they are actually writing. Real writers find a zone, get in a flow or a groove, and often resist any kind of disturbance. As you come to know your writers and their writing likes and dislikes, you will come to know the best time to chat with them about their writing processes—or you can just ask them.

Once you set the expectation that students will write more than you will ever read and more than they will ever be graded on, model what this daily independent writing looks like, and help students realize they do have valuable ideas they want to write about, independent writing time will begin to run smoothly as an instructional routine. Yes, some students will refuse to write. Others will want to write beyond the allotted class time. Remember, all students are at different places in their journeys to become accomplished writers. The authentic literacy teacher's primary task is to help every one of them advance even the tiniest bit forward. Daily independent writing time achieves this. Remember, the goal of authentic literacy instruction is to have students graduate as lifelong writers. Meeting this goal requires concerted, intentional effort and time to practice writing with an authentic literacy expert.

We intentionally mirror the language of the previous routine as we detail this one: to implement and sustain the routine of independent writing, teachers and students must be active participants. Setting the expectation that all students write about topics of their choice, try to apply skills-based lessons to their independent writing, and ultimately develop a habit of writing is a prerequisite for implementation, as is students' knowing the teacher will confer with them about their writing lives. Table 7.2 shows teacher and student actions that foster a habit of independent writing.

Table 7.2: Independent Writing—Activators for Deep Routine Implementation

Teacher Actions	Student Actions
• Providing texts that will ignite reaction in writers • Surveying the room, reinforcing the expectation for dedicated independent writing; redirecting as needed • Conferring with students about their independent writing, coaching when they get stuck, and helping them discover their own writing processes • Taking notes about feedback received from students during conferring • Monitoring student groups as they discuss their writing	• Writing independently • Responding to texts in a personal or text-based manner in their writers' notebooks • Composing other pieces, perhaps for publication • Holding peers accountable for quiet writing time once a community of trust is established • Conferring with the teacher about their independent writing or efforts to improve skills as writers • Sharing, listening, and giving feedback as they share writing in small groups

Conferring

The routine of conferring takes place in conjunction with independent reading and independent writing time. When you set a clear expectation that you will be meeting with individuals or small groups as students read or write, students might be timid at first, but most will respond positively to this personal attention, especially when it is targeted, specific, and personally relevant to their learning.

As described in chapter 6 (page 99), conferring is structured but flexible, planned but responsive. When teachers use conferring in tandem with self-selected independent reading (page 114), they dedicate these ten or fifteen minutes to personal conversation with readers, asking students to share portions of their reading or writing as evidence of their thinking, often via responses in their reader-writer notebooks (page 118). Teachers take notes from these conversations. Then, teachers, as individuals or with grade-level teams, can use formative conferring data to design responsive instruction for entire classes or small groups of students with similar identified needs. When they engage in conferring in tandem with students' independent writing time, teachers may reteach skills-based minilessons (page 119) specific to the writing task or review mentor texts (page 130) if students need additional support or ideas to help their process.

Conferring is a valuable, ongoing routine that supports building relationships with students, helping them take on the identities of readers and writers, and giving and receiving feedback. While teachers often initiate conferring conversations, students should do most of the talking so that teachers can collect feedback to ascertain learning needs and plan for instruction, scaffolding, or next steps. Listening is always more effective than lecturing. Table 7.3 shows teacher and student actions that foster a habit of conferring. Remember, the goal of authentic literacy instruction is to develop the habits of mind of real readers and writers who read and write beyond school. Conversations about books and writing ideas and processes are an essential step toward that goal.

Table 7.3: Conferring—Activators for Deep Routine Implementation

Teacher Actions	Student Actions
• Planning in advance to confer with two to four students per class period with the goal of reaching all students every two to three weeks • Keeping conferring notes, which may serve as valuable feedback needed to design further instruction or meet specific student needs • Modeling speaking with a lowered voice to limit disruption to other students' learning • Asking purposeful open-ended questions designed to engage students in conversation about their learning • Listening intently and responding in kind, validating student ideas, thoughts, goals, and needs	• Talking about reading and writing choices, thoughts, and processes • Asking questions regarding the task at hand or anything appropriately related to their reading or writing life • Directly referring to thoughts explored in their reader-writer notebooks or other assigned tasks • Setting learning goals and reflecting on the goals, progress toward those goals, and barriers in the way

Using Reader-Writer Notebooks

All experienced readers and writers recognize the messiness of their internal thoughts. While thinking is messy, readers and writers need a place to play with their tangled thoughts and ideas so those thoughts can take root and be fruitful. The reader-writer notebook, specifically devoted to recording ideas and inspirations and learning about reading and writing, is just that place. It's a place where writers can put their messy thoughts on the page and begin to sort them out—to discover beautiful ideas and things to say, discard thoughts that don't make sense, and collect thinking that isn't quite ready to be explored. The reader-writer notebook is also a place where readers can respond to and reflect on interactions with what they read. In turn, students use this tool as evidence of their thinking and learning during conferring conversations with teachers—owning their learning and articulating their growth in literacy skills.

The reader-writer notebook can be any notebook you, or your students, find suitable: physical, digital, or a mixture of both. We prefer composition notebooks for in-person class settings because they are sturdy and easy to stack, but other authentic literacy teachers find spiral notebooks meet their needs. For virtual learning, digital notebooks via Google Docs or Microsoft OneNote have proven useful.

This notebook facilitates students' ability to monitor their own progression of literacy acquisition throughout the year. It gives students a place to react and respond to a variety of texts, take notes on ideas and craft, and connect their reading and writing. Teachers must recognize this tool as owned by the students. This is an important distinction. If you want students to each use their reader-writer notebook authentically, you must honor and respect its content as part of the student's identity. This means that the reader-writer notebook is not a place for red ink (or ink of any other color) unless you have express permission from the writer to leave a mark on his or her page.

Reader-writer notebooks serve as powerful personal learning tools for readers and writers. These notebooks become a reference for past skills-based minilessons, a depository of ideas for writing, a place to record titles of books students want to read for self-selected independent reading (page 114), and a place for stress-free response writing (page 62) and other drafting. From a teacher's thinking aloud (page 124) to the reciprocal processes of reading and writing, students learn to use their notebooks to make their thinking visible and demonstrate their ability to apply minilessons, learn from mentor texts (page 130), and share their ongoing growth as readers and writers when conferring with the teacher (page 117) and collaborating with their peers (page 128).

Whether physical or digital, the reader-writer notebook is an ever-evolving resource that functions to help students collect, maintain, and expand on thinking. It bridges the expanse between reading and writing skills—a place to experiment and explore ideas and techniques to find what works and what isn't quite working yet. The reader-writer notebook is also a tool students use to respond to texts they encounter, through both personal and academic lenses. Table 7.4 (page 120) shows teacher and student actions to gain the most value from reader-writer notebooks.

Teaching via Skills-Based Minilessons

Students need clarity on what they're learning when they apply literacy skills independently and collaboratively; they need to know the criteria for success. The skills-based minilesson, a short burst of direct instruction, provides clarity for learning a specific literacy skill and models what application of the skill will look like when students turn to their independent work. Teaching skills-based minilessons based on ELA standards ensures alignment to the curriculum and provides focused direct instruction to the whole class or small groups, often while students study a mentor text (page 130) as a tool for applying their learning. Collaboratively crafted anchor charts, which are later displayed on the wall or recorded in reader-writer notebooks, can serve as references for independent work and criteria for success.

Readers, writers, and communicators seek ways to improve their skills, and a focused minilesson teaches a specific literacy skill—be it reading, writing, listening, or speaking—in a way students may immediately apply it. Authentic literacy teachers turn to their standards as a source for which skills to teach in these short yet impactful lessons. Pacing guides may prove helpful in determining when to teach them. Teachers also pay attention to their students' strengths and areas for improvement. Some authentic literacy teachers find it helpful

Table 7.4: Using Reader-Writer Notebooks—Activators for Deep Routine Implementation

Teacher Actions	Student Actions
• Thinking and writing beside students • Displaying a personal reader-writer notebook and modeling its use—showing thinking and writing on the page, including errors, revisions, and edits • Helping students organize their reader-writer notebooks so they can be functional tools for learning • Referring to the work and ideas students have in the reader-writer notebooks during conferring sessions • Providing feedback in a student's notebook when it is requested	• Keeping lists, setting goals, and reflecting on learning • Taking notes, cocreating anchor charts, and outlining personally inspired graphic organizers • Drafting written responses and other compositions • Playing with written language and specific techniques through imitation, response, and writing for discovery • Reading their writing in collaborative groups to share ideas, practice communication skills, and give and receive feedback • Seeking express feedback from the teacher when warranted

to work in grade-level teams as they plan minilessons. They examine student data (assessment performance, work samples, classroom observations, conferring notes, and so on) and design targeted instruction that addresses students' needs for growth in literacy skills. Assessment on students' application of skills-based minilessons provides measurable data, helpful for further instructional planning.

To teach a minilesson with staying power, you will want to model, think aloud, and cocreate anchor charts detailing student input, which record the lesson for students to view as they practice applying the skill. You'll also want to use appropriate texts that lend themselves to the skill you're teaching. As you practice planning minilessons and then executing them, your confidence will grow, and you will see the benefit of this direct teaching in a succinct and learner-centered form. Each day, establish a learning intention centered on a specific reading strategy, writing move, research practice, or language convention that supports students' growth toward proficiency in essential standards. When you teach minilessons at the beginning of a class period, teacher modeling sets this intention while you allow students to see and immediately apply the integrated processes for critical thinking, authentic reading, and reflective writing. Ideally, limit minilessons to between five and fifteen minutes to allow ample time for shared and independent practice afterward. Some lessons will take much longer than fifteen minutes to teach, so use your best judgment, and remember adolescent patience is limited, so the quicker you can teach something, the more engaged many students may stay.

Often, you must review and reteach minilessons, and sometimes, students need one-on-one instruction. By conferring with students, tuning into students' literacy needs, and listening to their conversations, you may notice a skills-based need you have not previously considered. Responsive teaching is vital: an authentic literacy expert learns how to read the room and respond to these student needs via minilessons on the fly. For example, say students are working on argumentative essays, and your planned minilesson is on supporting claims with effective examples. As you confer with writers, however, you notice that several of them have weak claims. You may want to take a step back and teach a minilesson on how to write strong ones. You may even find it effective to teach two whole-class minilessons that day.

In short, skills-based minilessons are the way authentic literacy teachers deliver clear expectations for student learning and model success criteria for literacy lessons. They last five to fifteen minutes, in most cases, and planning should happen in advance. There are two primary types of minilessons: (1) standards-based ones, possibly created in collaboration with grade-level teams, and (2) responsive ones, based on the immediate needs of students in the classroom. Both require teachers and students to think through literacy processes and immediately practice the lesson taught, independently or in small groups. Table 7.5 details the teacher and student actions for practical and purposeful direct instruction and learning via skills-based minilessons, and the following sections present two examples of skills-based minilessons.

Table 7.5: Teaching via Skills-Based Minilessons—Activators for Deep Routine Implementation

Teacher Actions	Student Actions
• Referring to past learning to elicit prior knowledge • Explicitly stating the point of the learning for the lesson (for example, "I want you to know ________" or "Today, we will learn how to ________") • Modeling thinking, reading, and writing skills • Using a text as a mentor, model, or anchor for a shared reading experience and as a learning tool • Cocreating anchor charts • Monitoring student collaboration and application of the skill taught	• Focusing on the teacher and perhaps keeping a record of the specific skill being taught and taking notes on the process in their reader-writer notebooks • Listening intently, knowing the expectation that they will practice independently • Reading along with the excerpt, mentor text, model, or sample writing • Cocreating anchor charts • Referring to anchor charts if needed during practice application • Sharing with partners or small-group members

Minilesson for Readers—Mood

To prepare for this reading minilesson on mood, find two excerpts from books in your classroom library to use as mentor texts that include a description that creates a significant mood. Most likely the author will have used colorful adjectives or imagery. Tell students that the focus for this lesson is on determining mood, which is how the reader feels about what he or she reads or the emotion he or she feels while reading. Tell them they will be expected to know how to determine mood in passages they read independently. Explain to students you are going to share a passage and ask them to help you determine what mood the author creates. Display one of the passages and read the passage once all the way through in order to gain the author's intended effect. Now, read the passage again, thinking aloud through how you determine mood. What do you notice about the word choice, or the sentence structure? Does the author use any figurative language? What does the imagery make you feel? Consider marking the text as you think through and answer these questions. Allow students to contribute to the analysis by sharing what they notice about the choices the author makes as well. Then, come to a consensus as a class on what the mood of the passage is. Next, on chart paper, begin creating an anchor chart titled "Determining Mood," and record the language choices you and the students noticed that helped you figure out the emotion the author intends for the reader. Hang the anchor chart on the wall. Then, give students the second selected passage to read in small groups as they work together to use the same line of questioning to determine the mood. Return to the anchor chart and add any other features the students noticed and used to determine the mood of the second passage. For independent practice applying the skill of determining mood, you can ask students to find a descriptive passage in their self-selected books to apply what they learned from this lesson.

Minilesson for Writers—Sentence Variety

In preparation for this writing minilesson on sentence variety, find a passage from a book in your classroom library that contains a nice variety of sentence structures. Tell students today's minilesson is about how writers use a variety of sentence structures to convey ideas. When writers vary their sentences, they often create a rhythm with the language; they are able to string ideas together to make their writing more concise; and they are able to draw attention to ideas that might be more important than others. Tell students you will expect them to apply what they learn about sentences in their own independent writing. Explain to students that you are going to display a passage, read it aloud, and ask them to pay attention to how the author crafts the sentences. Read the passage once all the way through to model fluency. Then, read the passage again, sharing your thinking about what you notice about the syntax. Depending on the passage you choose, consider commentary like "I see here this short sentence is surrounded by longer ones. That draws my attention to the short sentence." Or "I notice this sentence is long, and it seems to have multiple ideas within it." Then, mark the page noting the multiple ideas. You might say, "I wonder if it would change the meaning or rhythm of the sentence if the ideas were broken up into their own sentences." Or "I notice the author has used several dashes instead of just periods and commas. It seems like the dash tells me whatever follows it is important." Next, on chart paper, begin creating an anchor chart titled "Varying Your Sentences," and record the various sentence types you and your students notice in the passage you read. Next, ask students to turn to a page in their self-selected books and find other sentence structures you have not discussed yet. Add these to the anchor chart. For independent practice applying a variety of sentences in their writing, you can have students return to a previously written response and have them rewrite it using different, more varied syntax.

Billy's Reflections From the Field

My first year of teaching, I walked into the school building during the in-service week, before students' first day, looking for my classroom and trying desperately to gather whatever resources might help me teach my freshman and sophomore ELA students. My department chair approached me and declared that she had just the thing for me: a solid set of English textbooks.

The orange book covers were stained with shades of brown and bronze (from many snack-encrusted fingers, or blood—god, I hope it was snacks). These textbooks weighed twenty-three pounds, had been rudely cut at the top-right corner for identification to dissuade theft, and were as sticky and morbid as could be. I was surprised that these were my source for instruction, and I wasn't interested in what I saw.

Five days later, I quickly discovered that my students weren't interested either, and they never became interested in these dinosaurs for the five years I spent at that campus—a campus full of students who desperately needed to see themselves in the texts that I put in front of them. But they didn't. Because I didn't. Because I didn't have the means. Because I didn't have the expertise.

After a full two years of teaching—years in which I was inundated with full-on test-alignment pedagogy—I felt like I could figure it out. The problem was the *it* I was consumed with figuring out was the test, not the students. The problem was all my leaders, mentors, and peers identified the test as the important thing. Except for one person.

Stephanie Cash was the reading teacher on campus. She didn't have a classroom of her own but floated from classroom to classroom, teaching the learners who were often the hardest to teach: the "low" students, the English learners, the "bad" students, the students who couldn't read. And she was good at it!

Stephanie knew that students needed to read and read a lot. She knew that they wouldn't read unless they had access to books that they could read and wanted to read. She knew that her students needed daily access to books that interested them, called to them, mirrored them. So every day, as I stood inviting my students into a classroom that was obsessed with the wrong *it*, Stephanie floated past me in the hallway on the way to her next classroom, guiding a massive cart brimming with an eclectic variety of colorful novels—novels that made me curious.

I couldn't contain my curiosity, so one day, I asked her what she was doing with all those books. I'll never forget her explaining to me with a friendly laugh, "Billy, if we want kids to get better at reading, then we need to help them really read—and be able to do it for fun every day! Will you help me advocate for more money allocated to buy more books like these for your classroom?"

I feel shameful about how dismissive I was of Stephanie, her ideas, and her challenge to me that day. I wasn't anywhere close to understanding, or even hearing, the message she was modeling—that authentic reading should return to the classroom.

It took years and at least seven other distinct individuals and interactions to wake me up to the truth I ignored for so long after this interaction with Stephanie. My awakening was slow. But I promise you, yours doesn't have to be.

continued ▶

Once you accept that you can do better with authentic literacy instruction, and you know that this new understanding doesn't have to be accompanied with shame, embarrassment, or feelings of failure at how you taught in the past, you can move forward into a dynamic reformation of the learning experience you offer every student in your class every day.

Realizing that you've had the wrong *it* for two years or twenty doesn't have to be a catastrophe; it can be a liberating awakening, if you let it. Teachers need to look back on their prior selves and stances, then name and own up to them. Repair the damage when you have the opportunity.

The truth that Stephanie understood, and I didn't yet, was simple: I was getting in my students' way. All the test-aligned materials I was masterfully placing at their fingertips only impeded their ability to see reading, writing, and thinking as useful beyond school or the test I continued to talk about. I wasn't allowing my students' experience in my classroom to be an extension and empowerment of who they were.

Thinking back, I recognize this as a tragedy. I wish I had known a better way at the time, but I know I've learned from my errors.

Thinking Aloud

Teachers make complex thinking visible and model the kind of thinking they want students to adopt by thinking out loud through reading and writing processes: "The act of teacher modeling and thinking aloud allows students to see inside the mind of the teacher to discover how decisions are made" (Fisher et al., 2016, p. 53). The ultimate goal is to develop students' identities as authentic readers and writers. Modeling the skill students need to practice and making your thinking visible is the most important part of any skills-based minilesson, or any lesson for that matter. Doing this regularly supports students as they take ownership of their learning and make choices as readers and writers in critical, self-aware, and self-evaluative ways. You might think aloud to demonstrate how you select a book you might want to read, how you determine the tone or theme of a text, how you identify an idea you want to explore in your writing, how you combine sentences to make a more powerful thesis statement, and so on. When teachers think about their thinking and let students in on it, they teach students how to think about their own thinking—and the thinking that may be required to actually learn and apply a specific skill.

Here's an example scenario of what a think-aloud might look like in action. The teacher uses an excerpt from Neal Shusterman's (2016) novel *Scythe* to teach students to recognize that writers make arguments when they write, even in a novel. Holding up a copy of the book (or projecting a picture of the cover), the teacher says:

> *"Today, we're going to read an excerpt from* Scythe *by Neal Shusterman. In fact, we're reading the first page together."*

The teacher passes out copies of the first page (or directs students to download an electronic file on their devices).

> *"This book is the first of a three-book series. It's sci-fi about a future world in which society has eradicated many evils—but as a result, other problems have arisen.*

> *"One thing I want you to know is that writers, even in fiction, are constantly making arguments about big ideas and issues that relate to the real world—even our lives. As readers, we need to notice these arguments and think deeply about them—maybe even argue back in our heads and in written responses. Doing this will help us more thoroughly understand the deeper themes and understandings about the world and ourselves that the writer wants us to take away from the book.*
>
> *"So read along and even take notes about subtle, or not-so-subtle, arguments being made in this excerpt while I read it out loud."*

The teacher begins reading aloud. At one point, the teacher breaks from reading to say:

> *"So, I notice almost right away, in the second paragraph, the writer presents a pretty direct argument. In the first paragraph, the writer is using a narrator to tell us that, in the world of this book, innocent people are killed. And then, in the second paragraph, the narrator tries to explain the notion of being 'innocent' when it says:*
>
>> And as I see it, they're all innocents. Even the guilty. Everyone is guilty of something, and everyone still harbors a memory of childhood innocence, no matter how many layers of life wrap around it. Humanity is innocent; humanity is guilty, and both states are undeniably true. (Shusterman, 2016, p. 3)
>
> *"Before I analyze this argument, I need to remember something: writers use tools to talk to us readers. Here, the writer is using a narrator to bring us into the world of this book and help us understand the conflicts that are present. So as to the arguments I'm noticing, there's this idea that everyone is somewhat guilty of something but also innocent to some degree—that being human is something like a coin with two sides. And even though the two sides of that coin are completely different from each other, they are both still the reality: humans are good and bad at the same time . . . no escaping it. OK, let's keep reading and see if this argument is explained more, or if new arguments come up."*

Now, you may be wondering, "What's the difference between a minilesson and a think-aloud?" That's a good question, and in all practicality, the two are difficult to separate. Every effective minilesson requires that a teacher make his or her thinking visible; however, not every think-aloud necessarily involves teaching a skill. For example, say you are working to ignite student interest in a new stack of books you've acquired for your classroom library. You might choose to introduce these books by talking about their narrators. You might read the first paragraph aloud and then share your thinking: "I like this narrator because as I read, I thought __________ and __________." Or with another book, you might share, "I'm not sure I will like this narrator because as I read, I thought __________, and I didn't really get it until I read that part again." You've shared your thinking, but you have not specifically taught a skill as you would in a skills-based minilesson.

Here's another example: say your students have each drafted a persuasive essay. You've written beside them, and you project your writing so students can read it along with you.

As you read, you say aloud why you made the choices you did as a writer. Perhaps you ask for help by saying something like, "Do you see my shift in ideas between the first two paragraphs? I don't think my transition here really works. It seems rough and a little too vague. Will you help me think through it and come up with a transition that works better?" In this think-aloud, you've accomplished a few things.

- You've modeled the importance of rereading one's writing with the intent of revising to make it better.
- You've reminded writers they should have clear and smooth transitions between paragraphs.
- You've shown how a writer asks for help.
- You've made your thinking visible.

But as with the previous example, you have not explicitly taught a minilesson. If you so desired, you could transform this think-aloud into a minilesson by pulling out some mentor texts, studying how the writers transition between their paragraphs, and then asking students to independently apply that learning in their own drafts.

Thinking aloud teaches students what thinking sounds like—it voices what teachers want students to do as they make choices as readers and writers. Authentic literacy teachers capitalize on thinking aloud while talking about books students might choose for self-selected independent reading (page 114) or turning to their reader-writer notebooks (page 118) and sharing their writing and what thinking provoked the choices they made as they wrote. Teachers also think aloud as they teach skills-based minilessons (page 119) and study mentor texts (page 130), modeling how readers read and comprehend texts and how writers read texts in order to improve their own writing. Table 7.6 details the teacher and student actions for thinking aloud.

Thinking aloud to a room full of secondary learners can be intimidating; consider "Making Your Thinking Visible" to prepare you for this important instructional move.

Table 7.6: Thinking Aloud—Activators for Deep Routine Implementation

Teacher Actions	Student Actions
• Narrating thought processes aloud while making choices about books to read, topics to write about, and how to craft meaning • Reading texts aloud, or viewing them, and adding commentary, such as questions and answers • Marking or annotating texts in front of students • Monitoring student participation in discussions during minilessons to ensure thinking aloud helps students understand and learn the skills modeled	• Reading along or viewing a text, following along as the teacher shares commentary • Thinking about their own thinking as the teacher models his or hers • Marking or annotating a text to make their own thinking visible

Reader Reflection: *Making Your Thinking Visible*

Think about specific skills your readers need as they develop their reading identities. What are some ways you can share aloud the thinking you've done that has helped you develop as a reader?

-
-
-

Think about specific skills your writers need as they develop their writing identities. What are some ways you can share aloud the thinking you've done that has helped you develop as a writer?

-
-
-

Think about one specific skill in your standards, either reading or writing focused. Imagine what a think-aloud on this skill might look like in action and write a script for it.

Visit ***go.SolutionTree.com/literacy*** *for a free reproducible version of this reflection.*

Collaborating

An authentic literacy classroom is built on community and relationships (see chapter 3, page 37). This community depends on collaborative opportunities for learning—peer to peer, teacher to students, and students to teacher. For students to effectively collaborate, authentic literacy teachers model what collaboration looks like—such as the language and body language that readers and writers intent on growth use while interacting with others. Ideally, this modeling should occur as you set the expectations for a classroom based on community, sharing, and relationships at the beginning of the year, but as students shift small groups and new learners arrive in the classroom, refreshers that remind students how to collaborate effectively will be in order. Opening space for discussion around what actions take place in this kind of environment and explicitly noting what kind of language fosters trust in a community will help collaborative learning take root and thrive. You may consider facilitating productive academic discussions through various grouping strategies, as well as sharing protocols and supports, such as sentence stems, which often help students feel comfortable speaking.

One way to model collaboration is through the cocreation of anchor charts. For example, if you start the year with a discussion on the expectations you have for the learning community, you might have students create an anchor chart that captures the class's determinations as to what actions must happen in every class period to achieve those expectations. These charts are useful resources for ongoing learning, and they can be created with the whole class or in small groups.

Authentic literacy teachers model language that leads to collaboration and ask students to turn and talk with one another. This collaborative thinking is essential for building and sustaining relationships and community—and for establishing a culture where all students believe they can, and will, grow as independent readers, writers, and communicators. Talk is essential to authentic literacy instruction. Students should have multiple opportunities to collaborate with peers, in a variety of formats, on a daily basis. Often, collaboration involves talking and sharing with peers about reading and writing processes and goals. This can be done through partner, small-group, or whole-class interactions. Peer-to-peer collaboration can also take place virtually, with the proliferation of online platforms such as Google Classroom, Office 365, Zoom, Flipgrid, and other options. Remember, speaking and listening skills need equal space in your instructional routines. Inviting talk, which leads to collaborative thinking, opens this space. It also allows you to listen in on student discussions, which can provide important feedback as you plan next steps in your instruction.

Now, lest you think your students will quickly get off topic, never fear—they will! They are socially inclined teenagers after all. This is where your expertise comes into play. You must effectively and efficiently read the room and know when to redirect them and when to transition into the next instructional routine. That's not new to authentic literacy teachers—that's just good teaching.

Collaborative authentic literacy practices foster verbal engagement by providing students with ample time and structure to engage in productive academic conversation with peers in a safe and secure environment. As students read and experiment with writing style, they need sufficient time to work with each other in applying the skills from the minilesson, shaping meaning, refining ideas, and giving and receiving feedback. As they read self-selected independent reading books and study mentor texts and model essays, they need a chance to work together on identifying tone, making connections, analyzing theme, and teaching one another about their books and learning. As authentic literacy teachers guide students in this work as a literacy community, students grow in their confidence as readers and writers. They more willingly share, and they often start to hold one another accountable.

However, a safe learning environment is a prerequisite for any type of collaboration. By teaching effective discussion protocols—or setting norms—and then actively monitoring student talk, moderating debate, redirecting as necessary, and balancing talk time, teachers protect students' rights to be heard and respected. Authentic literacy teachers value and prioritize student talk, while concurrently recognizing learners need focus, structure, and guidance. Whether students work with partners, in small groups, or even as a whole class, collaborating helps them distribute the learning load, learn from and teach each other, take small risks in sharing new ideas with their thinking partners, and move the learning from direct instruction to guided practice.

Collaborating may include students' turning and talking to share titles of books they have chosen for self-selected independent reading (page 114) or topics they might want to explore in their independent writing (page 115). Or it may include students' giving and receiving feedback on assigned tasks, discussing global topics as they relate to mentor texts (page 130), or clarifying the *hows* and *whys* as they apply skills taught in skills-based minilessons (page 119). Remember, while reading and writing might appear to be solitary tasks, most readers and writers outside of school talk to other people about their reading and writing.

A major goal for collaborating is giving students the opportunity to grow their capacity to interact with and share ideas in a community of learners. Prior to implementing this routine, authentic literacy teachers must organize the classroom environment to facilitate collaborative work, including, when possible, seating students in partnerships or small groups. If facilitating virtual learning, consider assigning reading or writing partners or small groups. Table 7.7 outlines the teacher and student actions to ensure collaboration is successfully embedded in their instructional routines.

Table 7.7: Collaborating—Activators for Deep Routine Implementation

Teacher Actions	Student Actions
• Modeling the kind of thinking collaborators do when focused on a shared task, including using language that is kind and honest and respects vulnerability • Teaching protocols for discussion • Monitoring ongoing partnerships and small groups to determine progress toward goals, promote the balance of talk and production, and collect feedback • Revising instruction as needed	• Taking turns talking and listening to thinking partners • Sharing reading and writing thoughts, ideas, and processes in an open and vulnerable way • Giving and receiving feedback among peers with kindness, honesty, and positive presuppositions • Using language that feeds learning forward • Holding oneself and others accountable • Seeking the teacher's help or assistance when warranted

Using Mentor Texts

As described in chapter 5 (page 83), mentor texts serve as tools to help ELA teachers integrate reading and writing processes. Authentic literacy instruction focuses on the needs of individual readers and writers and offers choice as much as possible; however, studying mentor texts is a routine worthy of whole-class instruction. Studying them as a class shows learners the reciprocal nature of literacy skills as they move beyond reading like readers—to read for pleasure, comprehension, analysis, connection, and response—and into reading like writers—to craft writing for an audience that might read for pleasure, comprehension, analysis, connection, and response.

When teachers use texts that students read together for comprehension and analysis, often called *anchor texts*, students read like readers. They seek understanding of an author's meaning. When teachers use texts as *mentors*, noticing, studying, and analyzing the moves writers make to create meaning, students read like writers. They look for ways to apply authors' writing moves—be they structure, syntax, figurative language, repetition, or any number of other rhetorical or literary techniques or devices—in their own writing. In essence, using texts as mentors in an authentic literacy classroom empowers students to transfer what they learn as readers to skills they employ as writers. A beautiful thing about authentic literacy instruction is that anchor texts and mentor texts can be the same texts. Effective, beautifully crafted writing works to develop reading skills as well as writing skills.

Mentors can be complete texts (stories, articles, poems, or essays) or short excerpts (passages, paragraphs, sentences, or even phrases), and teachers can curate collections of excerpts from books or other texts they are reading. Mentors can also be video clips, infographics, memes, or other forms of digital text. In fact, when teachers read (or watch) like writers, mentor texts tend to leap off the page. Plus, when you use excerpts from books in your classroom library as mentors, you have the bonus opportunity to talk about those books with the class in the hope that someone will choose to read them.

Often, the mentor text is an essential component within a minilesson (page 119) and provides students a clear, direct example of the instructional focus. When used within minilessons, mentor texts are relatively short and strategically chosen to demonstrate the effective use of a particular craft move, genre characteristic, or language convention. Teachers select mentors such as these from a variety of genres and purposefully use them to teach literacy skills for independent application.

Of course, mentor texts can have other uses besides within skills-based minilessons. For example, perhaps you design a unit that includes asking students to write an op-ed, an opinion piece that usually focuses on a current societal issue or event. You may want to curate a set of mentor texts that includes several different op-ed pieces by various writers on various topics. Studying these mentors can help students understand that, though they might write in the same form and even with the same purpose—in this case, to share an opinion that persuades—not all writers make the same choices. Some writers might begin with an anecdote, and others might end with one; some writers might use emotive language, and others might rely on nuance. When students study several mentor texts, written in the same form they are being asked to write, they often realize possibilities they have not previously thought of. They begin to think about making choices.

Studying mentor texts such as these may take more instructional time than the five- to fifteen-minute minilesson. That is OK. Depending on the length of your mentor text and the skills you teach using it, you may teach a series of minilessons, or you may spend a class period reading the mentor text for content, comprehension, and analysis, perhaps followed the next day by two minilessons allowing time for students to apply the learning in their own independent practice. In our experience, relatively short mentor texts engage secondary students more effectively than long ones. Once you know your students, you will be able to determine the mentor texts that will hold their attention so they learn the lessons you hope they will.

Studying mentor texts proves useful *throughout* the writing process, and you can return to it again and again to review or refresh individual students on the skills they need to apply or improve. Conferring with students regularly often reveals this need for a mentor text revisit. Well-chosen mentor texts are an authentic literacy expert's most trusted writing coach.

Studying mentor texts helps transition students' thinking from reading like a reader to reading like a writer with the goal of applying writing craft, techniques, and ideas in their own writing. Any well-composed text can be used as a mentor, and the world overflows with current, relevant, personally meaningful texts your students will engage with and respond to. Table 7.8 displays teacher and student actions to fully utilize, and learn from, mentor texts.

Table 7.8: Using Mentor Texts—Activators for Deep Routine Implementation

Teacher Actions	Student Actions
• Collecting and curating excerpts from self-selected independent reading that can be used to teach specific skills throughout the writing process • Collecting and curating mentor texts from other reading, including articles, essays, poems, videos, and song lyrics, that can be used to teach specific skills throughout the writing process • Modeling by reading aloud, thinking aloud, and experimenting with writing imitation • Rereading and reusing mentor texts for multiple and different teaching objectives	• Reading along as the teacher reads the text aloud • Writing beside the mentor text—thoughts, annotations, questions, ideas, and so on • Noticing how independent reading texts can serve as mentor texts for writing • Imitating and applying writing craft and techniques • Practicing the skills that the teacher used the mentor text to teach

Summary

Creating new, more effective outcomes as an ELA teacher requires changes in your thought processes and plans for how and what you will teach. This chapter presented proven routines that are doable for every literacy teacher: opening space for self-selected independent reading and independent writing, conferring, using reader-writer notebooks, teaching in short bursts of direct instruction (minilessons), actively thinking aloud, selecting interesting and relevant mentor texts, and using these resources to develop the identities of every student reader and writer as they collaborate within the community.

We imagine two ways to make these routines work. The first is to take baby steps by selecting one routine as described in this chapter and implementing it however you can make it fit in your current instructional model and timeline. Then, select another and another until you've mastered all of them. Just remember, you will have to leave some of those current instructional models and timelines behind in order to make space for new routines that form more authentic habits of mind. The second way to make these routines work and truly transform your practice is to revolutionize your classroom in one fell swoop by implementing all eight student-centered routines. Either way you choose, you will begin a more authentic classroom that creates real readers and writers. You may stumble (we all have), but you'll learn (like we all have).

Your Turn: Chapter 7

Reflecting on what you've learned in this chapter, record your primary action steps. As an authentic literacy teacher, I will:

-
-

In one of the first history books ever written, ***History of the Peloponnesian War*** (originally written around 400 BCE), Thucydides (1972) recounts a debate among Athenians that included this argument: "A city is better off with bad laws, so long as they remain fixed, than with good laws that are constantly being altered" (p. 213). Here, Thucydides highlights two sides of a debate that has raged throughout history: Is it better to have a fixed system or a flexible one? This debate still rages in the secondary literacy classroom as well.

It's our position that the answer is ***both are necessary***. Secondary literacy instruction needs systems for some amount of consistency, and it needs some level of incongruence because not everything nor every student fits exactly into a like place. We argue that the fixed parts of what can be accomplished in an authentic literacy classroom are the routines and habits we've outlined in this chapter, not the long-held ELA traditions focused on teacher control and canonical texts. We argue that the flexible, alterable parts of what can be accomplished in an authentic literacy classroom are the students and their lives, hopes, interests, aspirations, and choices.

Think about this balance between constancy and flexibility and then answer the following questions. Share your writing with your own community. This might be your family, colleagues, students, team, or book club group.

- What are some things you can employ in your literacy classroom that help maintain constant, predictable systems?
- What are some ways you can foster space for flexible and responsive teaching and learning in your literacy classroom?

EPILOGUE

As you ponder the state of events, issues, and emotions colliding in the world, we hope you will join us in advocating for more humane relationships and authentic instructional practices within the walls of schools. Every ELA teacher has the opportunity to be a change agent and provide instruction that can help students not just navigate the world they live in but also seek out and find solutions for the problems within it. Literacy means more than it ever has before, and being fully and confidently literate can provide young people better access and better opportunities than ever before. The youth in ELA classrooms beg to be engaged. They seek answers to personal and global issues. And by and large, they want their teachers' trust just as teachers should be seeking theirs. Authentic literacy's implications for learning, growth, and human interactions are crucial to students' individual futures—and to society as a whole. It may not be in an English teacher's job description, but you can arm young people with powerful literacy skills and the abilities to become advocates for compassion, equity, courage, equality, justice, integrity, service, and peace—and what better weapons and healing balms than words?

As a teacher keen on student success, you must be willing to step into uncertainty and trust yourself as you make decisions that influence the lives of your most precious commodity, your students. Teachers can do more in schools and in ELA classrooms to help students engage, create, problem solve, take risks, and grow as capable and socially responsible individuals—all through the actions of authentic literacy teachers who understand the *who* is at the heart of their teaching. What better place than secondary English classes to practice what it means to be better humans?

While educational literacy standards, curricula, resources, and mandates have long focused on content and grammar, authentic literacy instruction focuses on the young humans in the classroom. What do they need to know their voices are heard? How can they make choices about their learning? How can you, as a teacher, spark motivation and capitalize on personal interests? Most important, how can you know your students will leave you firm in their identities as accomplished readers, writers, and communicators?

Authentic literacy instruction provided by an expert literacy teacher in a community of learners held to high expectations is the answer to all these questions. And it begins by taking one step and then another and another as you advance your authentic literacy action plan.

You are not alone in wanting more and better learning for your students. Thousands of teachers and administrators across the world already embrace many if not all of these authentic literacy practices. The ripple effects of student choice in reading and writing continue to spread and swell; you are now part of a mighty wave that's changing secondary literacy education for the better. Jump on in. The water (and all the authentic learning) is fine!

Remember, teachers create hope. And hope is what humankind needs—that, along with literate, critically thinking, empowered individuals who can make choices that will make society a better place. Authentic literacy is the avenue that just might get it there.

APPENDIX

Mentor Text Recommendations for Response Writing, Craft Study, and Models

As you select texts (prose, poetry, video, graphics, and so on) to use with your students, remember to keep your purpose for selecting a specific text at the forefront of your planning. Will your text give students a reason to write a response? Will it provide examples of how a writer uses a particular literary or rhetorical device? Will it be an adequate tool to help you teach a particular skill your readers or writers need to learn to accomplish your objective? The following mentor texts are ones that have worked well with our students.

- *Flying Lessons and Other Stories* by Ellen Oh (2017)
- *Heart-Shaped Cookies* by David Rice (2011)
- *Brave the Page: A Young Writer's Guide to Telling Epic Stories* by Rebecca Stern and Grant Faulkner (2019)
- *Helium* by Rudy Francisco (2017)
- *Long Way Down* by Jason Reynolds (2017)
- *The Red Bandanna* by Tom Rinaldi (2016)
- *How I Resist: Activism and Hope for a New Generation* by Maureen Johnson (2018)
- *Breakfast on Mars and 37 Other Delectable Essays: Your Favorite Authors Take a Stab at the Dreaded Essay Assignment* by Rebecca Stern and Brad Wolfe (2014)
- *Behind the Song* by K. M. Walton (2017)
- *Life Sucks: How to Deal With the Way Life Is, Was, and Always Will Be Unfair* by Michael Bennett and Sarah Bennett (2019)
- *Fresh Ink: An Anthology* by Lamar Giles (2018)
- *Black Enough: Stories of Being Young and Black in America* by Ibi Zoboi (2020)
- *The Hero Next Door: A We Need Diverse Books Anthology* by Olugbemisola Rhuday-Perkovich (2021)

- *Hope Nation: YA Authors Share Personal Moments of Inspiration* by Rose Brock (2018)
- *Dear Bully: Seventy Authors Tell Their Stories* by Megan Kelley Hall and Carrie Jones (2011)
- *I Will Always Write Back: How One Letter Changed Two Lives* by Caitlin Alifirenka and Martin Ganda (2016)
- *Look Both Ways: A Tale Told in Ten Blocks* by Jason Reynolds (2019)
- *The Book of Awesome Women: Boundary Breakers, Freedom Fighters, Sheroes, and Female Firsts* by Becca Anderson (2017)
- *Our Stories, Our Voices: 21 YA Authors Get Real About Injustice, Empowerment, and Growing Up Female in America* by Amy Reed (2018)
- *Once Upon an Eid: Stories of Hope and Joy by 15 Muslim Voices* by S. K. Ali and Aisha Saeed (2020)
- *You Too?: 25 Voices Share Their #MeToo Stories* by Janet Gurtler (2020)
- *Artists, Writers, Thinkers, Dreamers: Portraits of Fifty Famous Folks and All Their Weird Stuff* by James Gulliver Hancock (2014)
- *The Book of Lists: The Original Compendium of Curious Information* by David Wallechinsky and Amy Wallace (2005)

Classroom Library Book Recommendations

As you build your classroom library, keep in mind our guidance for creating a literature-rich classroom (see Curating Robust Classroom Libraries, page 55): curate a diverse selection of books that students want to read. In this appendix, we suggest a number of specific books that we think secondary literacy teachers will find valuable.

YA Books We Recommend for Students

The following YA books are ones we've found useful in helping our own students discover personal answers and explore others' conflicts as they've come to enjoy reading.

- *The Poet X* by Elizabeth Acevedo (2018)
- *Forgive Me, Leonard Peacock* by Matthew Quick (2013)
- *Scythe* by Neal Shusterman (2016)
- *Dear Martin* by Nic Stone (2017)
- *The Crossover* by Kwame Alexander (2014)
- *The Hate U Give* by Angie Thomas (2017)
- *Long Way Down* by Jason Reynolds (2017)
- *I Am Not Your Perfect Mexican Daughter* by Erika L. Sánchez (2017)
- *SHOUT* by Laurie Halse Anderson (2019)
- *Children of Blood and Bone* by Tomi Adeyemi (2018)

- *Every Last Word* by Tamara Ireland Stone (2015)
- *Goodbye Days* by Jeff Zentner (2017)
- *American Born Chinese* by Gene Luen Yang (2006)
- *Looking for Alaska* by John Green (2005)
- *El Deafo* by Cece Bell (2014)
- *I'll Give You the Sun* by Jandy Nelson (2014)
- *Ghosts of Heaven* by Marcus Sedgwick (2014)
- *The Astonishing Color of After* by Emily X. R. Pan (2018)
- *Refugee* by Alan Gratz (2017)
- *Brown Girl Dreaming* by Jacqueline Woodson (2014)
- *Eliza and Her Monsters* by Francesca Zappia (2017)
- *Don't Ask Me Where I'm From* by Jennifer De Leon (2020)
- *Don't Get Caught* by Kurt Dinan (2016)
- *Amal Unbound* by Aisha Saeed (2020)
- *Warcross* by Marie Lu (2017)
- *Futuristic Violence and Fancy Suits* by David Wong (2015)
- *The Marrow Thieves* by Cherie Dimaline (2017)
- *The Song of Achilles* by Madeline Miller (2011)
- *Will Grayson, Will Grayson* by John Green and David Levithan (2010)
- *Far From the Tree* by Robin Benway (2017)
- *This Is My America* by Kim Johnson (2020)
- *Sadie* by Courtney Summers (2017)
- *Exit, Pursued by a Bear* by E. K. Johnston (2016)
- *Spin* by Colleen Nelson (2019)
- *Just Lucky* by Melanie Florence (2019)
- *My Totem Came Calling* by Blessing Musariri and Thorsten Nesch (2019)
- *When You Ask Me Where I'm Going* by Jasmin Kaur (2019)
- *Turtle Island: The Story of North America's First People* by Eldon Yellowhorn and Kathy Lowinger (2017)
- *Everything Beautiful Is Not Ruined* by Danielle Younge-Ullman (2017)
- *Optimists Die First* by Susin Nielsen (2017)
- *Darius the Great Is Not Okay* by Adib Khorram (2018)
- *The Surprising Power of a Good Dumpling* by Wai Chim (2020)
- *It Sounded Better in My Head* by Nina Kenwood (2020)

- *Catching Teller Crow* by Ambelin Kwaymullina and Ezekiel Kwaymullina (2019)
- *The Head of the Saint* by Socorro Acioli (2016)

Other Books We Recommend for Students

The following books are ones outside the realm of YA that we've found helpful in engaging, and often challenging, our student readers.

- *Just Mercy* by Bryan Stevenson (2014)
- *Educated* by Tara Westover (2018)
- *Shoe Dog* by Phil Knight (2016)
- *A Place to Stand* by Jimmy Santiago Baca (2001)
- *A Long Way Gone* by Ishmael Beah (2007)
- *Between the World and Me* by Ta-Nehisi Coates (2015)
- *Extremely Loud and Incredibly Close* by Jonathan Safran Foer (2005)
- *Where the Crawdads Sing* by Delia Owens (2018)
- *Sing, Unburied, Sing* by Jesmyn Ward (2017)
- *A Thousand Splendid Suns* by Khaled Hosseini (2007)
- *The Curious Incident of the Dog in the Night-Time* by Mark Haddon (2003)
- *Neverwhere* by Neil Gaiman (1997)
- *In the Garden of Beasts* by Erik Larson (2011)
- *Killers of the Flower Moon* by David Grann (2017)
- *Behind the Beautiful Forevers* by Katherine Boo (2012)
- *David and Goliath* by Malcolm Gladwell (2013)
- *Freakonomics* by Steven D. Levitt and Stephen J. Dubner (2005)
- *The Alchemist* by Paulo Coelho (1998)
- *Station Eleven* by Emily St. John Mandel (2015)
- *Never Let Me Go* by Kazuo Ishiguro (2005)
- *The Road* by Cormac McCarthy (2006)
- *Hunger* by Roxane Gay (2017)
- *Homegoing* by Yaa Gyasi (2016)
- *Caramelo* by Sandra Cisneros (2002)
- *The Namesake* by Jhumpa Lahiri (2003)
- *Little Fires Everywhere* by Celeste Ng (2017)
- *Kafka on the Shore* by Haruki Murakami (2005)
- *Lives of Girls and Women* by Alice Munro (1971)

- *The Power* by Naomi Alderman (2016)
- *Heavy* by Kiese Laymon (2018)
- *There There* by Tommy Orange (2018)
- *Speak No Evil* by Uzodinma Iweala (2018)
- *Devolution: A Firsthand Account of the Rainier Sasquatch Massacre* by Max Brooks (2020)
- *Norse Mythology* by Neil Gaiman (2017)

REFERENCES AND RESOURCES

Acevedo, E. (2018). *The poet X.* New York: HarperCollins.

Acioli, S. (2016). *The head of the saint* (D. Hahn, Trans.). New York: Delacorte Press.

Adeyemi, T. (2018). *Children of blood and bone.* New York: Holt.

Alderman, N. (2016). *The power.* New York: Little, Brown.

Alexander, K. (2014). *The crossover.* Boston: Houghton Mifflin Harcourt.

Alexander, K., Allyn, P., Beers, K., & Morrell, E. (2016, November 19). *Expert-to-expert on the joy and power of reading* [Panel discussion]. National Council of Teachers of English annual conference, Atlanta, Georgia.

Ali, S. K., & Saeed, A. (Eds.). (2020). *Once upon an Eid: Stories of hope and joy by 15 Muslim voices.* New York: Amulet.

Alifirenka, C., & Ganda, M. (with Welch, L.). (2016). *I will always write back: How one letter changed two lives.* New York: Little, Brown.

Allington, R. L. (2013). What really matters when working with struggling readers. *The Reading Teacher, 66*(7), 520–530.

Allington, R. L., & Gabriel, R. E. (2012). Every child, every day. *Educational Leadership, 69*(6), 10–15.

Anderson, B. (2017). *The book of awesome women: Boundary breakers, freedom fighters, sheroes, and female firsts.* Coral Gables, FL: Mango Publishing Group.

Anderson, L. H. (2019). *SHOUT.* New York: Viking.

Applebee, A. N., Langer, J. A., Nystrand, M., & Gamoran, A. (2003). Discussion-based approaches to developing understanding: Classroom instruction and student performance in middle and high school English. *American Educational Research Journal, 40*(3), 685–730.

Baca, J. S. (2001). *A place to stand: The making of a poet.* New York: Grove Press.

Bancroft, C., & Rabinowitz, P. (2014). Euclid at the core: Recentering literary education. *Style, 48*(1), 1–34.

Beach, R., & O'Brien, D. (2018). Significant literacy research informing English language arts instruction. In D. Lapp & D. Fisher (Eds.), *Handbook of research on teaching the English language arts* (4th ed., pp. 1–29). New York: Routledge.

Beah, I. (2007). *A long way gone: Memoirs of a boy soldier.* New York: Farrar, Straus & Giroux.

Bell, C. (2014). *El deafo.* New York: Amulet Books.

Benjamin, A. (2015). *The thing about jellyfish.* Boston: Little, Brown.

Bennett, M., & Bennett, S. (2019). *Life sucks: How to deal with the way life is, was, and always will be unfair.* New York: Penguin Workshop.

Benway, R. (2017). *Far from the tree*. New York: HarperCollins.

Bishop, R. S. (1990). Mirrors, windows, and sliding glass doors. *Perspectives*, *6*(3), ix–xi.

Boo, K. (2012). *Behind the beautiful forevers: Life, death, and hope in a Mumbai undercity*. New York: Random House.

Brock, R. (Ed.). (2018). *Hope nation: YA authors share personal moments of inspiration*. New York: Philomel.

Brontë, C. (2017). *Jane Eyre*. London: Macmillan Collector's Library. (Original work published 1847)

Brooks, M. (2020). *Devolution: A firsthand account of the Rainier Sasquatch massacre*. New York: Random House.

Button Poetry. (2015). *Rudy Francisco—"My Honest Poem"* [Video file]. Accessed at www.youtube.com/watch?v=dDa4WTZ_58M on March 2, 2021.

Cambourne, B. (1988). *The whole story: Natural learning and the acquisition of literacy in the classroom*. Auckland, NZ: Ashton Scholastic.

Chim, W. (2020). *The surprising power of a good dumpling*. New York: Scholastic.

Cisneros, S. (1991). *The house on Mango Street*. New York: Vintage Books.

Cisneros, S. (2002). *Caramelo*. New York: Knopf.

Clear Creek Independent School District. (2018). *Strategic plan—Clear Creek*. Accessed at https://www.ccisd.net/explore_c_c_i_s_d/strategic_plan on June 11, 2021.

Coates, T.-N. (2015). *Between the world and me*. New York: Spiegel & Grau.

Coelho, P. (1998). *The alchemist* (A. R. Clarke, Trans.). San Francisco: HarperSanFrancisco.

De Leon, J. (2020). *Don't ask me where I'm from*. New York: Atheneum Books.

Dickens, C. (1999). *Nicholas Nickleby*. New York: Penguin. (Original work published 1839)

Dickens, C. (2002). *Great expectations*. New York: Penguin. (Original work published 1861)

Dickens, C. (2003a). *Oliver Twist*. New York: Penguin. (Original work published 1838)

Dickens, C. (2003b). *A tale of two cities*. New York: Penguin. (Original work published 1859)

Dickens, C. (2004). *David Copperfield*. New York: Penguin. (Original work published 1850)

Dimaline, C. (2017). *The marrow thieves*. Toronto, ON, Canada: DCB.

Dinan, K. (2016). *Don't get caught*. Naperville, IL: Sourcebooks Fire.

Doghonadze, N., & Kerdikoshvili, N. (2012). Planning in education and student-centered teaching. In L. G. Chova, A. L. Martínez, & I. C. Torres (Eds.), *Conference proceedings of the 5th International Conference of Education, Research and Innovation* (pp. 3315–3321). Madrid, Spain: International Association of Technology, Education and Development.

DuFour, R., DuFour, R., Eaker, R., Many, T. W., & Mattos, M. (2016). *Learning by doing: A handbook for Professional Learning Communities at Work* (3rd ed.). Bloomington, IN: Solution Tree Press.

Eastman, B. (2019, June 5). "It's the first time I've read a book with a character struggling like me" [Blog post]. *Three Teachers Talk*. Accessed at https://threeteacherstalk.com/2019/06/05/its-the-first-time-ive-read-a-book-with-a-character-struggling-like-me-guest-post-by-billy-eastman/ on April 22, 2021.

Fisher, D., Frey, N., & Hattie, J. (2016). *Visible learning for literacy, grades K–12: Implementing the practices that work best to accelerate student learning*. Thousand Oaks, CA: Corwin Press.

Fisher, D., Frey, N., & Hattie, J. (2017). *Teaching literacy in the visible learning classroom, grades 6–12*. Thousand Oaks, CA: Corwin Press.

Fisher, D., Lapp, D., & Whitmore, K. F. (2018, November 18). *What's new in the 4th edition of the* Handbook of Research on Teaching the English Language Arts*?* [Conference session]. National Council of Teachers of English Annual Convention, Houston, Texas.

Florence, M. (2019). *Just lucky*. Toronto, ON, Canada: Second Story Press.

Foer, J. S. (2005). *Extremely loud and incredibly close*. Boston: Mariner Books.

Francisco, R. (2017). *Helium*. Minneapolis, MN: Button Poetry.

Gaiman, N. (1997). *Neverwhere*. New York: Avon Books.

Gaiman, N. (2017). *Norse mythology*. New York: Norton.

Gay, R. (2017). *Hunger: A memoir of (my) body*. New York: Harper.

Giles, L. (Ed.). (2018). *Fresh ink: An anthology*. New York: Crown.

Gladwell, M. (2013). *David and Goliath: Underdogs, misfits, and the art of battling giants*. New York: Little, Brown.

Goodreads. (n.d.). *Joseph Campbell quotes*. Accessed at www.goodreads.com/quotes/314842-the-job-of-an-educator-is-to-teach-students-to on September 2, 2020.

Gorlewski, J., & Gorlewski, D. (2014). Context, codes, and cultures: An interview with NCTE president Ernest Morrell. *English Journal, 103*(4), 12–15. Accessed at https://secure.ncte.org/library/NCTEFiles/Press/Morrell_EJ.pdf on July 10, 2020.

Graham, S. (2018). Writing: Research and practice. In D. Lapp & D. Fisher (Eds.), *Handbook of research on teaching the English language arts* (4th ed., pp. 232–260). New York: Routledge.

Grann, D. (2017). *Killers of the flower moon: The Osage murders and the birth of the FBI*. New York: Doubleday.

Gratz, A. (2017). *Refugee*. New York: Scholastic.

Graves, D. H. (1983). *Writing: Teachers and children at work*. Portsmouth, NH: Heinemann.

Graves, D. H. (2003). *Writing: Teachers and children at work* (20th anniversary ed.). Portsmouth, NH: Heinemann.

Green, J. (2005). *Looking for Alaska*. New York: Dutton.

Green, J. (2019). *Turtles all the way down*. New York: Penguin.

Green, J., & Levithan, D. (2010). *Will Grayson, Will Grayson*. New York: Dutton.

Gunn, L. (n.d.). *The promise of who*. Accessed at https://www.thepromiseofwho.org/home.html on June 24, 2021.

Gurtler, J. (Ed.). (2020). *You too?: 25 voices share their #MeToo stories*. New York: Inkyard Press.

Guthrie, J. T., & Wigfield, A. (2018). Literacy engagement and motivation: Rationale, research, teaching and assessment. In D. Lapp & D. Fisher (Eds.), *Handbook of research on teaching the English language arts* (4th ed., pp. 57–84). New York: Routledge.

Gyasi, Y. (2016). *Homegoing*. New York: Knopf.

Haddon, M. (2003). *The curious incident of the dog in the night-time*. New York: Doubleday.

Hall, M. K., & Jones, C. (Eds.). (2011). *Dear bully: Seventy authors tell their stories*. New York: HarperTeen.

Hancock, J. G. (2014). *Artists, writers, thinkers, dreamers: Portraits of fifty famous folks and all their weird stuff*. San Francisco: Chronicle Books.

Hattie, J., & Clarke, S. (2019). *Visible learning: Feedback*. New York: Routledge.

Hattie, J., & Donoghue, G. M. (2016). Learning strategies: A synthesis and conceptual model. *NPJ Science of Learning, 1*. Accessed at https://www.nature.com/articles/npjscilearn201613 on June 24, 2021.

Hosseini, K. (2007). *A thousand splendid suns*. New York: Riverhead Books.

Ishiguro, K. (2005). *Never let me go*. New York: Knopf.

Ivey, G., & Fisher, D. (2006). *Creating literacy-rich schools for adolescents*. Alexandria, VA: Association for Supervision and Curriculum Development.

Iweala, U. (2018). *Speak no evil*. New York: Harper.

James, V. (2017). *Gilded cage*. New York: Del Rey Books.

Johnson, K. (2020). *This is my America*. New York: Random House.

Johnson, M. (Ed.). (2018). *How I resist: Activism and hope for a new generation*. New York: St. Martin's Press.

Johnston, E. K. (2016). *Exit, pursued by a bear*. New York: SPEAK.

Johnston, P. H. (2004). *Choice words: How our language affects children's learning*. Portland, ME: Stenhouse.

Kaur, J. (2019). *When you ask me where I'm going*. New York: Harper.

Kearney, M. (2001). Creed. In *An unkindness of ravens: Poems* (p. 72). Rochester, NY: BOA Editions.

Kenwood, N. (2020). *It sounded better in my head*. New York: Flatiron Books.

Khorram, A. (2018). *Darius the great is not okay*. New York: Dial Books.

Kittle, P. (2008). *Write beside them: Risk, voice, and clarity in high school writing*. Portsmouth, NH: Heinemann.

Kittle, P. (2013). *Book love: Developing depth, stamina, and passion in adolescent readers*. Portsmouth, NH: Heinemann.

Knight, P. (2016). *Shoe dog: A memoir by the creator of Nike*. New York: Scribner.

Kohn, A. (1993). *Punished by rewards: The trouble with gold stars, incentive plans, A's, praise, and other bribes*. Boston: Houghton Mifflin.

Kohn, A. (1999). *The schools our children deserve: Moving beyond traditional classrooms and "tougher standards."* Boston: Houghton Mifflin.

Kohn, A. (2018). *Punished by rewards: The trouble with gold stars, incentive plans, A's, praise, and other bribes* (25th anniversary ed.). Boston: Houghton Mifflin.

Koyczan, S. (2013, February). *To this day . . . for the bullied and beautiful* [Video file]. Accessed at www.ted.com/talks/shane_koyczan_to_this_day_for_the_bullied_and_beautiful?language=en on March 2, 2021.

Kwaymullina, A., & Kwaymullina, E. (2019). *Catching teller crow*. New York: Penguin.

Lahiri, J. (2003). *The namesake*. Boston: Houghton Mifflin.

Lake, N. (2012). *In darkness*. New York: Bloomsbury.

Laminack, L. L., & Wadsworth, R. M. (2015). *Writers are readers: Flipping reading instruction into writing opportunities*. Portsmouth, NH: Heinemann.

Lapp, D., & Fisher, D. (Eds.). (2018). *Handbook of research on teaching the English language arts* (4th ed.). New York: Routledge.

Larson, E. (2011). *In the garden of beasts: Love, terror, and an American family in Hitler's Berlin*. New York: Crown.

Laymon, K. (2018). *Heavy: An American memoir*. New York: Scribner.

Lee, H. (1960). *To kill a mockingbird*. Philadelphia: Lippincott.

Levitt, S. D., & Dubner, S. J. (2005). *Freakonomics: A rogue economist explores the hidden side of everything*. New York: Morrow.

Lu, M. (2017). *Warcross*. New York: G. P. Putnam's Sons.

Mandel, E. S. J. (2015). *Station eleven*. New York: Knopf.

Maxwell, J. (2019, December 3). *What are you reflecting on?* [Blog post]. Accessed at www.johnmaxwell.com/blog/what-are-you-reflecting-on on January 7, 2021.

McCarthy, C. (2006). *The road*. New York: Vintage Books.

McDowell, M. (2020). *Teaching for transfer: A guide for designing learning with real-world application*. Bloomington, IN: Solution Tree Press.

McLaughlin, M., & DeVoogd, G. (2018). Reading comprehension, critical understanding: Research-based practice. In D. Lapp & D. Fisher (Eds.), *Handbook of research on teaching the English language arts* (4th ed., pp. 85–109). New York: Routledge.

McLean, C., Prinsloo, M., Rowsell, J., & Bulfin, S. (2018). Toward a new appreciation of listening and speaking. In D. Lapp & D. Fisher (Eds.), *Handbook of research on teaching the English language arts* (4th ed., pp. 110–129). New York: Routledge.

McMurry, M. (2017, May 18). *Shane Koyczan—"Beethoven"* [Video file]. Accessed at www.youtube.com/watch?v=ppwowTJg0mI on March 1, 2021.

Miller, M. (2011). *The song of Achilles*. New York: Bloomsbury.

Muhammad, G. (2020). *Cultivating genius: An equity framework for culturally and historically responsive literacy*. New York: Scholastic.

Munro, A. (1971). *Lives of girls and women*. New York: McGraw-Hill.

Murakami, H. (2005). *Kafka on the shore*. New York: Vintage Books.

Murray, D. M. (1972). Teach writing as a process not product. *The Leaflet*, *71*(3), 11–14.

Murray, D. M. (1982). *Learning by teaching: Selected articles on writing and teaching*. Montclair, NJ: Boynton/Cook.

Musariri, B., & Nesch, T. (2019). *My totem came calling*. Toronto, ON, Canada: Mawenzi House.

Nelson, C. (2019). *Spin*. Toronto, ON, Canada: Dundurn.

Nelson, J. (2014). *I'll give you the sun*. New York: Dial Books.

Newkirk, T., & Kittle, P. (Eds.). (2013). *Children want to write: Donald Graves and the revolution in children's writing*. Portsmouth, NH: Heinemann.

Ng, C. (2017). *Little fires everywhere*. New York: Penguin.

Nielsen, S. (2017). *Optimists die first*. New York: Wendy Lamb Books.

Ogle, R. (2019). *Free lunch*. New York: Norton.

Oh, E. (Ed.). (2017). *Flying lessons and other stories*. New York: Crown Books for Young Readers.

Orange, T. (2018). *There there*. New York: Knopf.

Owens, D. (2018). *Where the crawdads sing*. New York: G. P. Putnam's Sons.

Pan, E. X. R. (2018). *The astonishing color of after*. New York: Little, Brown.

Pearson, P. D., & Lopez, M. L. (2018). Epilogue. In D. Lapp & D. Fisher (Eds.), *Handbook of research on teaching the English language arts* (4th ed., pp. 451–463). New York: Routledge.

Piercy, M. (2011). Where dreams come from. In *The hunger moon: New and selected poems, 1980–2010* (p. 317). New York: Knopf.

Quick, M. (2013). *Forgive me, Leonard Peacock*. New York: Little, Brown.

Raines, A. S. (2005). Louise Rosenblatt: An advocate for nurturing Democratic participation through literary transactions. *Talking Points, 17*(1), 28–31.

Rasmussen, A. (2016, December 8). Better teaching: Please tell me your story [Blog post]. *Three Teachers Talk*. Accessed at https://threeteacherstalk.com/2016/12/08/better-teaching-please-tell-me-your-story/ on April 22, 2021.

Rasmussen, A. (2018, December 4). Conferring and my wish for a time machine [Blog post]. *Three Teachers Talk*. Accessed at https://threeteacherstalk.com/2018/12/04/conferring-and-my-wish-for-a-time-machine/ on April 22, 2021.

Rasmussen, A. (2019, May 7). Four things I wish I'd known when I became an English teacher [Blog post]. *Three Teachers Talk*. Accessed at https://threeteacherstalk.com/2019/05/07/four-things-i-wish-id-known-when-i-became-an-english-teacher/ on April 22, 2021.

Rasmussen, A., & Eastman, B. (2018). An intervention change-up: Investing in teacher expertise to transform student learning. *English Journal, 107*(4), 26–32.

Reed, A. (Ed.). (2018). *Our stories, our voices: 21 YA authors get real about injustice, empowerment, and growing up female in America*. New York: Simon Pulse.

Reynolds, J. (2016). *As brave as you*. New York: Atheneum Books.

Reynolds, J. (2017). *Long way down*. New York: Atheneum Books.

Reynolds, J. (2019). *Look both ways: A tale told in ten blocks*. New York: Atheneum Books.

Reynolds, J., & Kiely, B. (2015). *All American boys*. New York: Atheneum Books.

Rhuday-Perkovich, O. (Ed.). (2021). *The hero next door: A We Need Diverse Books anthology*. New York: Yearling.

Rice, D. (2011). *Heart-shaped cookies*. Tempe, AZ: Bilingual Press/Editorial Bilingüe.

Rief, L. (2019). What's next in writing must be what was in writing. *Voices From the Middle, 26*(4), 31–34.

Rinaldi, T. (2016). *The red bandanna*. New York: Penguin.

Robbins, A. (2008). *Unlimited power: The new science of personal achievement*. New York: Simon & Schuster.

Saeed, A. (2020). *Amal unbound*. New York: Puffin Books.

Sánchez, E. L. (2017). *I am not your perfect Mexican daughter*. New York: Knopf.

Sedgwick, M. (2014). *Ghosts of heaven*. New York: Roaring Brook Press.

Shusterman, N. (2016). *Scythe*. New York: Simon & Schuster.

Sinek, S. (2009, September). *How great leaders inspire action* [Video file]. Accessed at www.ted.com/talks/simon_sinek_how_great_leaders_inspire_action?language=en on January 7, 2021.

Skerrett, A., & Warrington, A. (2018). Language arts instruction in middle and high school classrooms. In D. Lapp & D. Fisher (Eds.), *Handbook of research on teaching the English language arts* (4th ed., pp. 410–435). New York: Routledge.

Stern, R., & Faulkner, G. (2019). *Brave the page: A young writer's guide to telling epic stories*. New York: Viking.

Stern, R., & Wolfe, B. (Eds.). (2014). *Breakfast on Mars and 37 other delectable essays: Your favorite authors take a stab at the dreaded essay assignment*. New York: Roaring Brook Press.

Stevenson, B. (2014). *Just mercy: A story of justice and redemption*. New York: Spiegel & Grau.

Stone, N. (2017). *Dear Martin*. New York: Crown.

Stone, T. I. (2015). *Every last word*. New York: Hyperion.

Summers, C. (2017). *Sadie*. New York: Wednesday Books.

Szymborska, W. (1998). Possibilities. In *Poems, new and collected, 1957–1997* (S. Barańczak & C. Cavanagh, Trans.; pp. 214–215). New York: Harcourt Brace.

Tan, A. (2005). *Saving fish from drowning*. New York: G. P. Putnam's Sons.

Thomas, A. (2017). *The hate u give*. New York: HarperCollins.

Thomas, A. (2019). *On the come up*. New York: HarperCollins.

Thucydides. (1972). *History of the Peloponnesian War* (M. I. Finley, Ed., & R. Warner, Trans.). London: Penguin. (Original work published 4th century BCE)

Tovani, C. (2016, June 10). *Do-overs and second chances: Helping students revisit reading and writing* [Conference presentation]. North Texas Council of Teachers of English Language Arts Conference, Hurst, Texas.

University of Wisconsin–Madison School of Education. (2018, January 22). *Jason Reynolds on book haters* [Video file]. Accessed at www.youtube.com/watch?v=6fFmiHWltlQ on January 7, 2021.

Verghese, A. (2010). *Cutting for stone*. New York: Vintage Books.

Waack, S. (2018, October 12). *Collective teacher efficacy (CTE) according to John Hattie*. Accessed at www.visible-learning.org/2018/03/collective-teacher-efficacy-hattie on June 7, 2021.

Wallechinsky, D., & Wallace, A. (2005). *The book of lists: The original compendium of curious information*. New York: Canongate Books.

Walton, K. M. (Ed.). (2017). *Behind the song*. Naperville, IL: Sourcebooks.

Ward, J. (2017). *Sing, unburied, sing*. New York: Scribner.

Westover, T. (2018). *Educated*. New York: Random House.

Wiesel, E. (1960). *Night* (S. Rodway, Trans.). New York: Hill & Wang.

Wilhelm, J. D. (2015). Teaching texts to SOMEBODY!: A case for interpretive complexity. *Voices From the Middle*, *22*(4), 44–46.

Willingham, D. T. (2015). For the love of reading: Engaging students in a lifelong pursuit. *American Educator*, *39*(1). Accessed at www.aft.org/ae/spring2015/willingham on January 7, 2021.

Wong, D. (2015). *Futuristic violence and fancy suits*. New York: St. Martin's Press.

Woodson, J. (2014). *Brown girl dreaming*. New York: Penguin.

Wright, R. (1945). *Black boy*. New York: Harper.

Yang, G. L. (2006). *American born Chinese*. New York: First Second Books.

Yellowhorn, E., & Lowinger, K. (2017). *Turtle island: The story of North America's first people*. Toronto, ON, Canada: Annick Press.

Younge-Ullman, D. (2017). *Everything beautiful is not ruined*. New York: Viking.

Zappia, F. (2017). *Eliza and her monsters*. New York: Greenwillow Books.

Zemelman, S., Daniels, H., & Hyde, A. (2005). *Best practice: Today's standards for teaching and learning in America's schools* (3rd ed.). Portsmouth, NH: Heinemann.

Zentner, J. (2017). *Goodbye days*. New York: Crown.

Zoboi, I. (Ed.). (2020). *Black enough: Stories of being young and Black in America*. New York: Balzer + Bray.

INDEX

I'm Listening
Beth Pandolpho
Rely on *I'm Listening* to help drive deeper, more meaningful learning by integrating relationship building into lesson design. Using the book's practical strategies will help you empower learners to succeed at all subjects by being proficient readers, writers, speakers, and listeners.
BKF926

The New Art and Science of Teaching Writing & The New Art and Science of Teaching Reading
The New Art and Science of Teaching framework has helped educators around the globe transform instruction. Written by subject-matter experts, these content-specific books detail how to make the most of Dr. Robert J. Marzano's groundbreaking model in the areas of reading and writing.
BKF796 BKF811

Every Teacher Is a Literacy Teacher series
Written by acclaimed experts and practitioners, the *Every Teacher Is a Literacy Teacher* series details how to promote literacy growth across disciplines and grade bands. Learn how to build a common language, work in collaborative teams, implement literacy-infused instruction, and more.
BKF904 BKF907 BKF908

The Fundamentals of (Re)designing Writing Units
Kathy Tuchman Glass
Perfect for teachers, curriculum designers, and literary coaches, *The Fundamentals of (Re)designing Writing Units* provides guidance for designing new writing units and revising existing ones across content areas for grades 5–12. Discover practical strategies for teaching skills in drafting, editing, revising, feedback, and more.
BKF711

Literacy Reframed
Robin J. Fogarty, Gene M. Kerns, and Brian M. Pete
Discover a game-changing new way to think about—and teach—literacy at all levels. With *Literacy Reframed*, you will discover a dynamic path forward for creating classrooms that fully support students on their literacy journeys and prepare them to become lifelong lovers of reading.
BKF959